Managing the One-Person Library

CHANDOS
INFORMATION PROFESSIONAL SERIES

Series Editor: Ruth Rikowski
(email: Rikowskigr@aol.com)

Chandos' new series of books is aimed at the busy information professional. They have been specially commissioned to provide the reader with an authoritative view of current thinking. They are designed to provide easy-to-read and (most importantly) practical coverage of topics that are of interest to librarians and other information professionals. If you would like a full listing of current and forthcoming titles, please visit www.chandospublishing.com.

New authors: we are always pleased to receive ideas for new titles; if you would like to write a book for Chandos, please contact Dr Glyn Jones on g.jones.2@elsevier.com or telephone +44 (0) 1865 843000.

Managing the One-Person Library

Larry Cooperman

AMSTERDAM • BOSTON • HEIDELBERG • LONDON
NEW YORK • OXFORD • PARIS • SAN DIEGO
SAN FRANCISCO • SINGAPORE • SYDNEY • TOKYO
Chandos Publishing is an imprint of Elsevier

CHANDOS
PUBLISHING

Chandos Publishing is an imprint of Elsevier
225 Wyman Street, Waltham, MA 02451, USA
Langford Lane, Kidlington, OX5 1GB, UK

British Library Cataloguing-in-Publication Data
A catalogue record for this book is available from the British Library

Library of Congress Control Number: 2014955914

ISBN: 978-1-84334-671-5

For information on all Chandos publications
visit our website at http://store.elsevier.com/

Typeset by Thomson Digital

Working together
to grow libraries in
developing countries

www.elsevier.com • www.bookaid.org

Dedication

To my wife Adrienne, my biggest supporter, with all my love.

Contents

List of figures

About the author

Larry Cooperman is currently an adjunct faculty librarian at the University of Central Florida in Orlando, and a national adjunct online instructor for Rasmussen College, teaching research and writing skills to upper-level business undergraduates. He has worked as a solo and small-library manager and director for the past ten years, primarily in academic, public, and school libraries.

He served on the Northeast Florida Library and Information Network Continuing Education Committee from 2002 to 2004 (serving as chair in his final year) and the Florida Library Association's Scholarship Committee from 2003 to 2006. He has presented a half-day workshop, IT Resources on the Internet, for librarians at various locations, and has taught his online course, Managing the One-Person Library, for Simmons Graduate School of Library and Information Science since July 2009. He also writes book reviews for *School Library Journal*, *Reference & User Services Quarterly*, *and College & Research Library News*; he received the Outstanding Achievement Award for Book Reviews from the Reference and Users Association of the American Library Association in May 2010 and May 2011. He also received the 2009/2010 Librarian of the Year Award from Everglades University.

Preface

For most of my library career I have managed small academic libraries for student populations of 600 and under, with some assistance from two or three students who covered the library and helped users when I was not available. Prior to that, I worked as an intern in a small corporate library. You could say that I thought other librarians who worked in groups or in larger libraries were the odd ones out!

Why did I become a solo librarian? I enjoyed learning different skills, such as cataloging, collection development, and reference, and liked being the librarian in charge. I never found a solo librarianship position lonely or difficult; I appreciated the challenge of learning new skills and managing a library successfully on my own. Many librarians become well versed at one skill, but I appreciated using my numerous skills when I managed solo libraries during my career. As a solo librarian, I usually was the go-to person or the point person, and not just for students and faculty. Management asked me to troubleshoot IT problems on the school's computers, for instance. I became responsible for any testing or teacher evaluations, as most of these took place online and most of the computers resided in the library. There were times when I needed to use my organizational skills to the fullest, as I was pulled in many directions by my patrons and management, but I overcame these problems and learned to become a good organizer and facilitator.

Figure P.1 Norwegian library, 1946: the "old" face of the library

When people think of a librarian, they usually think of a professional who works with other librarians in a public library, a school library, or a college library. Yet many librarians do work alone, some without any assistance from students or volunteers, and they successfully run and manage their libraries to serve their patrons, whether these are the public, a handful of students, or many students. These librarians cover a wide range of specialties, such as medicine, law, school, and business. They serve populations in large cities and small towns, with a wide range of users with different backgrounds, personalities, and occupations. Many library managers around the world may not have the credentials, such as a master's degree, that most professional librarians have earned, but these paraprofessionals, as is the main technical term for them, perform the same library management tasks as do their accredited counterparts. They need to have the same skills and strategies to manage their one-person libraries as their counterparts with a professional degree. Going forward in this book, to avoid confusion and unless otherwise noted, I include both professional and paraprofessionals as solo librarians.

Figure P.2 Bibliotheca Alexandrina, 2008: the "new" face of the library

There have been several books and articles dealing with solo library management, but I have not, in my career, noticed any books that use a personal or anecdotal approach to the topic, and I wanted to record my experiences as a solo librarian to assist other solo librarians in their work. I had created an online continuing education course several years ago, and realized that I could reach a larger audience of solo librarians with such a book and it would fill a niche that needs to be filled – that of an appreciation of solo library management and how to approach it successfully, whether those solo librarians are new to the field or veterans. I cover such topics as time management, circulation, cataloging, collection development, and professional development, with an emphasis on how solo librarians can enhance their services to their patrons, students, and customers and thrive on their own. I include many case studies from solo librarians, which will help readers to learn from the experiences of others so that they can combine these with their own knowledge and skills and learn new ones. Finally, I also include additional resources for further reading and reference.

Many librarians thrive in this environment and enjoy their work; this book will affirm their career choice and help them pursue their careers successfully.

Who is a one-person, or solo, librarian? And how do they manage to do what they do? 1

To start, it is obvious that a solo librarian (which term I will use going forward, as opposed to "one-person librarian") generally works by himself/herself (except for some assistants, whether they are students or library paraprofessionals). Solo librarians are responsible for managing all of the library functions that are usually handled by different departments in larger libraries, such as collection development, cataloging, and circulation. Library paraprofessionals without an advanced degree in library and information science, in many libraries around the world, perform the management tasks professional librarians do in other libraries. Solo librarians work in a variety of libraries – public, school, college, and corporate – where non-solo librarians also work. They serve a diverse group of people, whether they are public library patrons, students, instructors, business people, lawyers, or doctors, to name just a few. They work varied hours and may not always be available to help their patrons (and may have to rely on student workers or volunteers to fill in the gaps of time when they are not there). They may report to a manager or may just manage their own work schedule (probably the better and the ideal of the two!). But whatever their backgrounds, education, or type of libraries they manage, solo librarians differ from their counterparts in their responsibility for running the entire library and serving their patrons, clients, or students effectively and efficiently. Solo librarians must be everything and everyone to serve their clients well, whether they are physically present in their libraries or not. But how can they manage and function to serve their patrons well? Time management, organizational management, and change management skills can help solo librarians prioritize their tasks and allow them to run their libraries effectively on their own.

Time management

The eighteenth-century French chemist Antoine Lavoisier demonstrated that matter is always conserved, never destroyed – he never knew about time, evidently! Time is a resource that always seems to slip through our fingers; how can we as librarians manage our time more efficiently and effectively to serve our patrons better? Figure 1.1

Since the first studies of industrial workers' time a century ago, time management has been an important component of how efficient and effective workers can become by compartmentalizing and dividing their tasks. Now most solo librarians, as mentioned, must do a bit of everything to accomplish their work, so time management must help them to realize all of their tasks, not just some of these. Time management allows solo librarians to organize their work properly.

Figure 1.1 Swiss railway clock: time waits for no one

Some librarians may find time management to be confining and restrictive; they believe that they do not need to create a schedule covering every possible minute of their work day in order to feel fully organized and busy at all times. But time management does not have to be so all-encompassing; solo librarians should think of it as a skeleton to embellish later with bones, muscles, blood, and organs. It should be seen as a first step in organizing their daily schedules.

What did I do to start effective time management? My plan, after I realized what my daily job requirements and duties consisted of, was to write down my specific tasks. Then I would organize those daily tasks on certain days and at certain times. For instance, shelf readings could be conducted on a given day, and cataloging on a certain day or at a certain time of day when students were in class and I could give my undivided attentions to the joys of cataloging!

But what if some event or meeting or something out of the blue arrived and threw off my entire plan? The thing to remember is that a time management schedule needs to be flexible – as most librarians realize, when there is an emergency or crisis, they are the ones everyone turns to for help (my personal motto as a librarian is "in case of emergency, break glass!"). A good time management plan takes into account meetings, time out of the library, and any daily crisis (or crises) that may occur. Plans should not be etched in stone; for instance, if I received a book shipment (sometimes up to 15 boxes at a time) from my bookseller, I would revise my schedule to allow for processing and cataloging over a period of time – say several days. I would block off certain times during the day when I could devote most of my time to this task. I would divide a project like this one into doable tasks (I like to call this "chunking" a task). With chunking, I could make what seemed an insurmountable task surmountable.

Finally, an ideal time management plan should change daily; of what use is a fixed schedule when work schedules change so often? Most solo librarians (or any librarian, for that matter) arrive at work each day, create a to-do list, and prioritize the tasks that lie ahead of them. And since each day is different, it makes sense to have a general time management plan that allows for daily flexibility and change if the need arises. Time management can be summed up as follows.

*   Time management allows solo librarians to accomplish their daily tasks effectively and efficiently.
*   Time management plans should be flexible to allow for any changes in a solo librarian's schedule.
*   Time management plans should allow librarians to deal with their customers first.
*   Time management plans should vary daily to allow for changes in a librarian's tasks.
*   Each and every day, create a to-do list and prioritize that list with the most important task that needs to be completed on that day. Then prioritize other daily tasks in the order you think those tasks need to be handled. Always remember to check off a task when you have finished it – this may sound trivial, but I have found that checking off a finished task gives an enormous sense of accomplishment and spurs me on to complete the next task.
*   Break your larger tasks into smaller, more doable tasks that can be completed on a daily basis – this "chunking" makes an insurmountable task or project much easier to deal with (and keeps the hair on your head intact!). Small changes, such as chunking or checking off completed tasks, can give a solo librarian the confidence to organize and complete daily tasks and larger projects.

Now that we have established how important a time management plan is for solo librarians, how do we organize such a plan? The next section deals with organization management strategies to create successful time management plans.

Organizational management strategies

As noted, organizing and running a one-person library require good time management skills, perhaps more so than for librarians who work in conventional libraries. And successful time management skills require good organizational skills. How should solo librarians organize their time successfully? What are good organizational tools to use?

First, find an organizational method that you are comfortable with. I have noticed that there are two methods to organize schedules and projects – written or electronic. Some librarians not used to technology (or maybe just technophobes!) tend to favor the paper and the pen: they create to-do lists, they write reminders for themselves, they write dates and meeting times in a diary. In the other camp, technophile librarians will opt for Blackberries and smart phones to create their daily to-do lists and reminders about meetings. Other electronic methods, such as Excel spreadsheets or organizational tools such as Microsoft Outlook, are also effective organizational tools to create order out of chaos.

Which of the two is preferable? Neither – as I mentioned above, choose the organizational method you find more comfortable, and use it often. One advantage, however, of electronic methods of organization is their portability and their ability to store your work in them, allowing for editing, changing, or creating documents practically anywhere a solo librarian goes. Electronic devices such as smart phones also allow easy and frequent oral and written communication with others. There are numerous free applications for smart phones, such as EasilyDo, Evernote, and ifttt (short for "if this, then that"), which can help solo librarians manage their time. Most solo librarians can use these devices to organize information about their library budgets, acquisitions, shelf reads, and just about any other data needed to run a solo library (of course, circulation and cataloging information is usually found on a desktop or laptop library computer, but this information can easily be synched or downloaded on to a smart phone or other PDA if it is needed at a meeting or a conference, for instance). Solo librarians, I have noticed, are the ones who are interested in learning new technologies or changing their work and organizational habits, as they need to adapt and change in order to run their libraries more effectively. So if you are one of those solo librarians on the technophobic side, you may want to explore learning how to use technology to your advantage. I would suggest starting with one technology, like Microsoft Outlook, and then working your way up to other technologies. Websites like www.microsoft.com have numerous tutorials, both in PowerPoint and in audio formats, that allow you to learn a technology easily. Microsoft Outlook is a great organizational tool, with calendar and note features that allow a solo librarian not only to stay in touch with others but to organize files and messages easily. Even Google, the website that librarians love to hate, contains applications such as Google Now and Google Calendar to organize a solo librarian's time effectively and efficiently.

Nevertheless, a hybrid model of paper and computer can work for most solo librarians, as it allows for flexibility of use in different locations (in the library itself and while traveling or commuting). The important aspect of using good organizational tools is that they allow solo librarians more time to assist and help their patrons, as well as managing the library itself. The old adage of the poor workman blaming his tools is relevant here, as solo librarians need to find what type and what level of organization tools will help them manage their libraries effectively and efficiently.

Change management strategies

Many management books talk about the fact that change, whether it is in the company's hierarchy or in its policies or procedures, is a fact of life in most organizations, and many books detail how employees can embrace change to ensure a healthy and prosperous work environment for themselves and their co-workers. Librarians now use change management skills to implement new policies and procedures more effectively than in the past (Adedoyin et al., 2012; Kelly, 2010; Warnken, 2004). How can solo librarians maintain their management skills and professionalism amid changes in their organizations?

Solo librarians, as mentioned before, work in diverse settings – there are school librarians (both secondary and post-secondary), public librarians, law-firm librarians, medical librarians, and corporate librarians, to name a few. Change will occur in any organization, yet despite their differences, solo librarians embrace change in the same way, even though the types of change may vary. How is this so? Solo librarians are usually the sole managers of their workplace, so change affects them quickly; there are no buffers of other librarians or departments to allow change to affect them in a slower fashion. And perhaps no one feels the brunt of change more than the information facilitators and disseminators, the librarians!

From experience, I can say with comfort that change happens and moves faster in smaller organizations than in larger ones. And change, whether for good or for ill, can produce stress, anger, and other forms of negative behavior. What can a solo librarian do to manage organizational change in an effective manner?

There are two parts to understanding change management: power and reason. Power consists of change management strategies for leaders, and reason consists of implementing change when you, the librarian, are not in charge of a situation.

Now, power and reason here may sound like a contradiction in terms – how can you be in charge and not be in charge? But one-person librarians, I would like to propose, are in this paradoxical position: we lead and are led. So these change management parameters can truly help us, as solo librarians, to maintain our sanity and professionalism.

So a paradox has been stated – what can solo librarians do to embrace and grow in their professional development by change management? Here are some ideas.

- First, and perhaps foremost, maintain communication with your manager as well as your co-workers. Some organizations are very good at maintaining open communication between co-workers; others, I have noted, are very poor at this. Why is this so, when communication, as most good librarians know, is the life-blood governing how well organizations function? Perhaps to keep information from workers (to have more control over their work), perhaps from laziness... Whatever the reason, maintaining open lines of communication allows solo librarians to gain a semblance of control in their work and stay ahead of the curve when it comes to change and adapting to change.
- Second, learn to adapt to change. No one, in all honesty, likes change; most people like to continue to work in the same way they have always worked, completing their tasks in the same way they have always completed them. When change does arrive, most people throw their hands in the air and decide not to change at all, contemplating a stealth campaign against their employer to do it their way or no way at all. This is not a solution; a solution is to adapt to change gradually. Like chunking tasks, adapting to change gradually gives the appearance of change not being the daunting or impossible task that it seems to be. However, change may arrive rapidly, unannounced, and all at once – what is the solution here? Accept the change willingly and, again, try to chunk it so that you are not overwhelmed by it.
- Finally, solo librarians should take a leadership role in the organization when change occurs. Librarians are the gatekeepers and the disseminators of information, and a major part of change is good communication of those policies and procedures that are going to change. Disseminating information frequently and cogently, serving on committees dealing with the policy changes, and setting an example of positive change in the library are all good strategies of change management.

Change, like death and taxes, will always exist in the workplace and in our world; the key is to understand it, embrace it, and work with it in order to serve our patrons in the best way we can as solo librarians.

Stress management

Here I give some thoughts dealing with managing stress. Many librarians do find their work to be rewarding, yet very stressful. Solo librarians can find their work even more stressful, as they are the ones who run their libraries from the ground up; they are responsible for circulation, cataloging, collection development, budgeting, and inventory, to name some responsibilities. It is important to remember here that stress never disappears totally, but can, with the proper strategies, diminish somewhat and be managed somewhat to enable solo librarians to enjoy their work and their profession. Implementing the organizational and change management strategies mentioned earlier can help to alleviate stress. Beyond this, what else can solo librarians do to alleviate stress on the job, apart from the usual deep breaths and massages? Here are some additional tips.

- Take breaks during your day. This sounds like a time-worn and obvious tip, but a change of scenery from your library can work wonders in changing your mood and your attitude towards work. If you can find a replacement for a few minutes, such as a staff member, an instructor, or even a work-study student, leaving your post for a brief time can help you put a new perspective on your work and lessen any tension you may have when a crisis or a problem arises. These breaks are especially effective after a problem lands on your desk; leaving is a great way to cool down and see your work through a new set of eyes, a set that is not focused on the task at hand. There are some librarians who believe that their libraries will fall apart and collapse if they leave their posts even for a few minutes; do not believe them for a moment! Librarians are human beings, not robots, and everyone needs a break or two during the day to maintain their sanity.
- If possible, try to work with your supervisor or manager about changing schedules or work hours; this allows for a change of pace in your work (on some levels, it's like arriving at a new job!). Working different hours is not for everyone (some people like to adhere to the same schedule, and others, for reasons of the library they work for, cannot do this), but it's worth a try to change your schedule for a new perspective on how to run and manage a library.
- Attend as many professional development conferences or meetings as you can, depending, of course, on your schedule. This may be difficult, especially for school librarians who usually don't have back-up or substitutes to cover for them, but if you can do it, meeting other librarians in a professional setting, as well as learning a skill or two, is invaluable not only for professional development but for stress reduction – attending a meeting is an event to look forward to and therefore a stress reducer in its own right. Technology now affords us the professional webinar, so it is much easier for busy solo librarians to set aside a bit of time in their libraries to watch a webinar for an hour and not have to spend the time traveling away to attend professional conferences. Some may say that webinars aren't as satisfying as live conferences or meetings, as there is no face-to-face contact, but they are a great resource if you don't have a lot of time (or back-up) to leave your library. Podcasts serve a similar function as webinars; these technologies should definitely be embraced by those solo librarians who want to learn and to meet other librarians, but cannot leave their libraries due to either scheduling or other constraints (such as budgetary ones). I discuss professional development for solo librarians in more detail in Chapter 3.

People management

All librarians have to deal with stressful events and with people, whether they are patrons, customers, or students, to note some examples. Solo librarians, however, need to deal with certain people, such as managers, more directly than those who work in larger libraries. Solo librarians are usually the "go-to" people in many organizations, as they are the source of all information, not just from books and electronic databases. These can be tricky relationships at times, since the solo librarian not only has to answer to his/her users, but to a manager more directly and more frequently than non-solo librarians. A good relationship with a manager can make a big difference between a stressful workplace and a less stressful workplace. What can solo librarians do to maintain a good working relationship with their managers?

Be available

I am reminded of an old story attributed to the long-time Los Angeles Dodgers manager Tommy Lasorda. When he first played baseball in the minor leagues, he remembered seeing a billboard for condensed milk that read "contented cows give contented milk". He never forgot this advice as he led his teams to many National League pennants and World Series wins. And the same advice can be used by anyone who works for a manager – if you can help your manager or supervisor make her or his job a bit easier, you will be remembered by them for that. It is important not only to act professionally, of course, but to be there when they need help, and solo librarians will always need to be there and be ready to help, given they are the only librarian or information professional around in an organization.

Be ready to help and offer solutions

I recall the advice a library school professor had for us in his library management class – always offer a solution to a situation that arises. For instance, if you need to be away from your workplace during your library's scheduled opening hours, make sure you have coverage from a student or volunteer worker in your place. A manager will appreciate your doing so instead of just saying that you have to change your scheduled opening times and not having alternative cover. Having alternative plans goes a long way to establishing good relationships with managers; they will remember your doing so and can be more amenable to budgetary and other financial allowances, for instance. Of course, they may not have the funds available to help you or grant your requests, but being available, ready to help and to offer solutions to problems will go a long way to cementing a solid, long-term relationship with management.

Take the initiative

Everyone wishes to be acknowledged for the work they do in an organization. And what better way to receive such recognition than by taking the initiative as a solo librarian in volunteering for a project or assisting in other ways in your organization, in order not only to help with improving your organization or company, but also to enhance your profile and standing as a solo librarian? Doing so may reap benefits, such as more funding for your library maintenance and programs; there is no guarantee that such action will do so, of course, but a little goodwill on your part to help can go a long way in providing support from management for your library.

Case studies

Amanda Tarbet, reference librarian, MGH Institute of Health Professions, Boston, MA

Management Plan for the IHP Library, July 2013–June 2014

Part I: Setting Goals

The library's and individual librarian's goals for the upcoming year should be set at the conclusion of the previous fiscal year, ideally using the outcomes from the previous year as the basis for a new set of annual goals. Goals are subject to change depending on the overall organizational environment, and space will be made for adjustments as barriers or new ideas emerge. The goals that are set should be specific, realistic, and measurable.

The goals for the 2014 FY are as follows:

1. *Continue to provide effective reference services to students and faculty.*
   a. *Answer reference questions in a timely and professional manner.*
   b. *Update and maintain course reserves.*
   c. *Provide research consults or one-on-one instruction as needed.*
   d. *Develop and assess new and current classroom instruction sessions and workshops.*
2. *Create, update, and maintain various web services.*
   a. *LibGuides: Create new research guides as needed. Update current guides, checking for broken links, out-of-date resources.*
   b. *Video tutorials: Improve accessibility of current tutorials. Create new tutorials as needed.*
   c. *Website: Make updates as needed. Improve accessibility and usability.*
3. *Develop, maintain, and evaluate the physical collection.*
   a. *Acquire, process, and promote new materials.*
   b. *Evaluate, weed, and dispose of current materials as needed.*
   c. *Track and manage circulation of materials using ILS.*
4. *Market and promote library services to community members, as well as external organizations and associations.*
   a. *Reach out to community through newsletters, book groups, liaising with faculty, hosting events, and promo materials like custom bookmarks.*
   b. *Seek out and apply for appropriate grants.*
   c. *Participate in the greater LIS community through conference attendance, poster proposals, continuing education.*

Part II: Achieving Goals

Time and task management are integral to reaching organization and individual goals. For each goal and its tasks:

1. *Plan out the tasks and projects that will be necessary to reach a goal. Identify what actions need to be taken, whose assistance you may need, and evaluative measures.*

Carol Munroe, Milwaukee, WI Public Schools: The one-person library overall management plan

As I am working with a library with no systems in place, there are two possible perspectives: I have no change management to worry about (and cannot improve our systems for it) *or* I have the highest possible level of change (one that is open to infinite improvement).

Because I am starting from scratch, I have greater latitude in choosing what systems and set-ups we will use. At this point, I am operating in the belief that our best option is preparation for future changes, particularly in technology.

At present, I know that I will have both Microsoft Outlook and OneNote available to me. I already have used these two tools together very effectively in the past to track projects from inception to completion. The Outlook Task feature handles small or routine tasks. OneNote handles the bigger picture and keeps all necessary info aggregated.

So, with these things in mind, my change management plan looks roughly as follows.

- Keep abreast of industry trends, changes, and developments through formal publications, blogs, and listservs.
- Begin collecting information – positive and negative – to decide if a program or change of interest is worth pursuing.
- If yes, pull together a proposal for the director of instruction, principal, and superintendent; make sure it's well sourced.
- Go through any necessary rounds of research/present/revise (likely to include "how much will this cost?").
- Publicize and present proposal to those who would be affected; get their feedback. Adjust plans as necessary.
- If everyone's given input, the principal and director of instruction back the plan, and it's still looking like a good idea, go for it!

As a practical example, I hope to switch from Dewey to a genre-based system in three or four years. While we could theoretically open with such a system, I firmly believe that the students' input will be critical to making it work long term. So I will want to get the administration's approval, poll students about how they use the library and what would make it more useful them, and then, once all those data are collected, decide what looks like it will work and (hopefully) spend a very busy summer moving everything around.

The perk of working solo is that I'm not likely to have to argue about "what works best for everyone" when it comes to certain behind-the-scenes aspects of library management. If I want to run projects out of OneNote, I can – no disputes. The downside is that I have to research, pitch, plan, execute, and explain any changes largely on my own.

To summarize

- Successful time management strategies allow for solo librarians to budget their time wisely to serve their patrons more fully.
- Successful organizational strategies are the proper tools to use to create successful time management strategies.
- Change management strategies allow for solo librarians to thrive and to grow their libraries to serve their patrons well.
- Stress management strategies allow for solo librarians to stay focused in their work environments.
- Solo librarians need good people management skills to maintain good working relationships with their manager or supervisor.

I have demonstrated, in this chapter, some management strategies that can help solo librarians accomplish their work more effectively and efficiently; the next chapters deal with the actual management tasks that solo librarians face.

References

Adedoyin, Samuel Olu, Imam, Abayomi, and Bello, Taofik Olatunde (2012). "Management of change in 21st century libraries and information centres". *Library Philosophy and Practice*, February, 1–11.

Kelly, Tricia (2010). "A positive approach to change: the role of appreciative inquiry in library and information organizations". *Australian Academic & Research Libraries*, *41*(3), 163–177.

Warnken, Paula (2004). "New technologies and constant change: managing the process". *Journal of Academic Librarianship*, *30*(4), 322–326.

Further reading

Cook, Sarah and Macauley, Steve (2004). *Change Management Excellence*. Sterling, VA: Kogan Page.

Gilley, Ann (2005). *The Manager as Change Leader*. Westport, CT: Praeger.

Hines, Samantha (2010). *Productivity for Librarians: How to Get More Done in Less Time*. Oxford: Chandos Publishing.

Lawson, Ken (2007). *Successful Time Management*, Business Buddies Series. Hauppauge, NY: Barron's Educational.

Mackenzie, Alec and Nickerson, Pat (2009). *The Time Trap* (4th edn). New York: American Management Association.

Maktelow, James (2007). *Manage Your Time*, Work/Life Series. New York: DK Publishing. (This book is available on Amazon.com, but it appears to be out of print at this time. This is unfortunate, as it is an excellent pocket guide to time management, organization, and delegation; numerous helpful diagrams, charts, and photographs make for easy reading and, most importantly, retention!)

Roberto, Michael (2005). *Time Management: Increase Your Personal Productivity and Effectiveness*, Harvard Business Essentials Series. Boston, MA: Harvard Business School Press.

Marketing your library

2

There are dozens, probably hundreds, of books and articles on how to market your library, as well as numerous workshops, webinars, and associated paraphernalia. You may have read them or attended them, or you may not have done so. But they all have one important component that might not be mentioned – the librarian's motivation to market the library successfully.

If a solo librarian is motivated enough to want to market his or her library to be the best it can be (with apologies to the US Army's well-known slogan), then marketing the library is not an uphill battle. It may still be an enormous challenge, but with the proper motivation, successfully marketing a library can be accomplished.

Many librarians, and those not involved in the marketing business, consider marketing a selling or, worse, a huckstering tool to get people to purchase items they don't want or don't need. Some people find marketing beneath them, and either loath it or ignore it as a library activity. Many librarians believe that if you passively offer resources, whether they are books, electronic databases, or other library materials, patrons will come and use them. But librarians who ignore marketing their libraries and their resources do so at their own peril – there are many choices and options for people to find books or other information on the internet (including the dreaded Google and Wikipedia!). Many people may ask "Who needs libraries or librarians?" But librarians perform a distinct and important service, providing people with the proper information and the proper resources that they may not know are available to them – they are truly the information gatekeepers. So library marketing is essential to ensure that your customers (or your patrons, if you prefer that term – to me, they are interchangeable) know what you have available for them to use. Garoufallou et al. (2013) provide a comprehensive literature review of library marketing services, convincingly demonstrating to the library profession that marketing for any type of library is vital and necessary.

To begin with, let us clarify what marketing is. Marketing, according to *Webster's College Dictionary*, is "the process or technique of promoting, selling, and distributing a product or a service" (Merriam-Webster, 2011). Many librarians will most likely blanch at the word "selling" in this definition: a task that librarians will not do. But let us think differently for a moment – does selling here have to mean earning a commission or coercing a customer or patron to purchase an item they do not want or need? Not necessarily; in this case, "selling" in a library sense could mean to sell the patron use of an online reference service to borrow a book that they may not have thought of reading before. Does that involve any huckstering? Yes, it does, but it doesn't have to imply that a librarian is trying to hoodwink patrons into using services they don't need. Robinson (2012) strongly demonstrates that the ideas of Peter Drucker, one of the best-known business thinkers of the twentieth century, can be used to create

successful library marketing strategies. Librarians are using marketing ideas and strategies, as well as focusing on what their patrons need – and selling them those services,
even if the services don't cost any money to use. So selling is an extension of marketing – but librarians need to market their services so that their patrons are satisfied with
their experience in the library. And this satisfaction extends to more visits, more uses,
and (not always, but usually) budgetary funds to increase library usage. Jose and Bhat
(2007) stress the seven "Ps" of successful library marketing – product offer, price,
place, physical evidence, promotion, processes, and people. And even if budgets aren't
increased due to marketing, marketing is an activity that any librarian can and should
do – it is the life-blood of why one is a librarian, especially a solo librarian. It is the
means for our existence and our occupation.

Now that we have defined what is marketing, and how crucial it is for solo librarians to practice it, how do solo librarians market their libraries successfully?

Resources and strategies

When people think of marketing, they usually think of large, expensive campaigns
involving a lot of time and money and effort that a solo librarian usually does not have.
Marketing products and some services generally does involve this effort, but library
services usually are not in this category. In fact, marketing can be run on a very limited
budget. How can this be accomplished?

The simplest way that solo librarians can market their services is by word of mouth.
Simply getting away from behind your desk or in your office and helping students on
an individual basis is the best way that solo librarians can connect with their students,
help them, and market their services. A solo librarian need not have all the fancy
electronic databases or the most books available for checkout – a solo librarian need
only possess the drive, the intelligence, and the passion to provide excellent services
for patrons. Once patrons see that a librarian is helping them (or at least trying to help
them), they should (but, of course, do not always) continue to use your library's resources (which include yourself!) and tell their colleagues the same.

Successful word-of-mouth campaigns also extend to a solo librarian's presence
in her/his institution or workplace (Barber, 2014). If solo librarians just come in to
work and keep their heads down and sit in their offices, no one, including management, will notice them and use their services. It is imperative that librarians, in addition to helping their patrons, take an active role in their organizations. Volunteer
your time on a committee or a charity that you enjoy, offer to conduct research
for a department, and use your services resourcefully and successfully – these are
simple, yet very effective, ways for management and the rest of your colleagues
to take notice of your work. Granted, you may receive more work than you wish
to obtain or can accomplish (don't take on too much that you cannot handle!), but
assist your organization by offering your knowledge and your resources – doing so
can only give you needed exposure and generate goodwill and (perhaps) financial
benefits that will allow you to provide even more services, not only to your patrons
but to your colleagues as well.

Another way to raise your visibility is to go outside your library – actively educate your patrons, whether they are students or co-workers, about the resources you have available in your library (as well as your own expertise, which is a valuable resource in itself!). This education experience can consist of a short Power-Point or Prezi presentation of available resources or can be a live tour of your library and its resources, yourself included (e.g. research consultations). The main point here is to get away from behind your desk and out of your office and connect with your patrons – they will put a name to the face and a face to what you have available to help them when they need assistance in their studies or office work. Here, action is an even more potent marketing tool than just word of mouth; actively demonstrating your resources to your patrons shows them what you actually do, as opposed to just handing them a brochure on your available resources. And it is important to maintain this relationship of connecting with your patrons on a regular basis: provide them with updated resource lists, new books available in your library, and specific, useful websites in their fields of study or work – this can easily be accomplished with regular emails to your patrons (made a lot simpler if you have a smaller library, which most solo librarians do have). This is one of the benefits of running a smaller library; you can personalize your service a lot more easily than a larger library. And a personalized reference or research service will usually result in your patrons turning to you again if they need assistance.

If possible, given space and time constraints, make your library available to other groups in your organization; for instance, if you can hold a book group or studying or tutoring group in your library, do so. Libraries are (and should remain) havens of peace and quiet, but sometimes they can become too quiet and underused, and seen by many as a place not conducive to some interaction with patrons. Hosting these events will demonstrate to your patrons that a library can be a living place where they are welcomed (and those who may not have heard of your services and your resources may use them as a result of the library's openness to the organization). If at all possible, try to give the community access to your library; there may be impediments and reasons for not allowing the community to use your resources, but if it is possible, exposure of your library to the community is just another way to market and to increase the visibility of your resources and your work.

As noted above, there are plentiful books available on successful library marketing, and many solo librarians, whether they are new or veterans, know of the many strategies to market their libraries and their services effectively – book displays, scavenger hunts, and open houses are just a few of the useful and resourceful ways of marketing libraries. What methods are there beyond these tried-and-true ideas? I have already mentioned maintaining communication with your patrons with email messages about new resources; for ambitious solo librarians, if they are able, how about creating and updating library websites so that your patrons are aware of any changes in resources that your library may have? How about creating Facebook or Twitter pages, or instant messaging for ease of communication with your patrons? How about advertising your library services with social media (Chan, 2012)? How about using library blogs to showcase your resources and services (Kaushik and Arora, 2012)? These communication tools are also useful in learning from your patrons what resources are needed in your library and what potential new services you can offer. It is important to show your patrons that you are interested in obtaining their opinions about what services they wish to have, not just what you propose to have. Communication makes a library conducive to their needs, as well as your needs.

Case studies

Amanda Tarbet, reference librarian, MGH Institute of Health Professions, Boston, MA

MGH IHP Community Health Library Marketing Plan, June 2013

1. *Mission Statement*
   a. *This is still being determined but will probably be about promoting community health by serving IHP and the wider Massachusetts community.*
   b. *Should clearly define the role of the library, the needs the library satisfies, and the benefits it provides. Should also include a distinctive competence that sets this library apart from others and an indication of future direction.*
2. *Summary of Performance*
   a. *Define our broad practices:*
      i. *What general services do we already provide?*
      ii. *What markets do we serve?*
      iii. *What types of marketing communications do we already use?*
   b. *SWOT analysis:*
      i. *Strengths.*
      ii. *Weaknesses.*
      iii. *Opportunities.*
      iv. *Threats.*
3. *Overall Assumptions*
   a. *Can make some assumptions based on what we already know about our services and how our patrons use them.*
   b. *These assumptions should be taken into account when making marketing (and other) decisions.*
4. *Audience*
   a. *Need demographics about who our broad community of users are.*
      i. *Students.*
      ii. *Faculty.*
      iii. *External community members (especially this group as we prepare to market the library to customers outside of the school).*
   b. *Then, need more specific data about who our core customers are.*
      i. *Surveys (online).*
      ii. *Focus groups?*
      iii. *Reference question and circulation statistics.*
   c. *Information we need from a community assessment:*
      i. *Who are our customers?*
      ii. *What do our customers want from us?*
      iii. *Why do our customers use us?*
      iv. *What do they use us for?*
   d. *Use above information to identify a "core" group of customers.*

5. *Overall Marketing Objectives and Strategies*
   a. *An objective is what you want to achieve and should be quantified.*
      i. *Assessments helped us to determine that our student core customers want a searchable catalog to make finding resources easier.*
      ii. *The OPAC is up and running but usage is low.*
      iii. *We want to increase use/traffic to the OPAC by 50% in the next academic year.*
   b. *A strategy is how you plan to achieve your objectives.*
      i. *Increase awareness of the OPAC by:*
        (1) *Visiting classrooms of those core customers most likely to use it and telling them about it face to face.*
        (2) *Visual displays by the physical location of the resources.*
        (3) *Notices on the library website and the LibGuide about the collection.*
      ii. *Measure awareness of the OPAC by:*
        (1) *Using web analytics to determine changes in OPAC traffic.*
        (2) *Analyzing ref question data to see if people have asked how to use the OPAC.*
6. *Budget*
   a. *Printing – $50 maximum.*
   b. *Web analytics – free to $10/month, depending on what we want from it.*
   c. *Total budget – $200 maximum.*

Lisa Lin, career resource consultant, McGill University Career Planning Service, Montreal, Quebec, Canada

Marketing Policy

Target Audience and User Profiles

Primary audience

Students and alumni. *Patrons come to the Centre for the following reasons: career exploration, job-seeking strategies, access to job and employer listings, work experience options, and career development in general. The Centre has identified and categorized the primary audience into five groups. The categorization is based on their needs rather than academic status (e.g. undergraduate, graduate, post-doc, alumni, etc.).*

- Group 1 – Graduating students. *Our most frequent users, most of them start using the resources in the Centre after seeing an advisor for a career question or CV review. Since this group is about to graduate, the motivation to visit the Centre and use the resources is high.*
- Group 2 – Students seeking work experience. *This group's main motivation to visit the Centre is to obtain work experience in the fields they major in. They are particularly interested in finding summer or volunteering opportunities.*
- Group 3 – Students seeking career options different from their majors. *Students of this group visit the Centre because they seek future career direction or answers to life. This group appears to feel lost and requires lots of emotional support.*

- Group 4 – Students planning for higher education. *This group visits the Centre for advice and information on graduate applications, personal statements, and standardized tests.*
- Group 5 – New students. *Students in this group are usually first-year university students. They are low-frequency users. The main reasons for the low visit rate that the Centre has identified include unawareness of the existence of the Centre, and lack of the concept that career planning is a lifelong process and should start at an early stage.*

Secondary audience

Career advisors or staff members. *Their main motivation for visiting the Centre is primarily for professional development. They seek resources such as the latest information on career advising/counseling skills, labor market information, resources they can direct students to in their advising sessions, and employer contacts for their career panels and workshops.*

Situation Analysis

Besides the programs and services, the Centre currently has in place the following marketing strategies.

- Social media (Twitter, Facebook, YouTube, Blog, LinkedIn). *Used for broadcasting upcoming events and introducing useful resources.*
- RSS. *The Centre posts monthly announcements to promote new acquisitions and resource-related freebies.*
- Announcement board. *For posters of upcoming events and advertisements from employers.*
- Flyers and resource cards. *They are placed in the Centre for students to take home.*

Strengths

- *The Centre is up to date with social media technologies.*
- *The Centre's location is highly visible when students walk in the Student Services building.*
- *The Centre's website contains rich information and resources.*
- *All the logos and graphics representing the Centre are standardized.*

Weaknesses

- *Social media are underutilized, especially with customer relationship building.*
- *Collaboration and communication with other units in Student Services are not quite established.*
- *The website needs to be organized in a way students can better find the information they need.*
- *With the budget cut, the marketing plan is heavily relying on low-cost marketing strategies.*

Marketing Strategies

Note: *For the purpose of this assignment, the strategies proposed are for "Group 5 – New Students".*
Goal: *Raise the awareness of the Resource Centre and its resources to new students.*
Expected outcome: *To increase usage of the resources in the Centre and potentially broaden base of users.*
Strategy 1: *Partner with other organizational units to promote the Centre.*
Objective 1.1: *Promote to students at the start of a student's university life.*
    Action 1.1.1: *Prepare a short description which can be included in the booklet that is a part of the new-student welcome package.*
    Action 1.1.2: *Prepare a brochure and distribute to the First-Year Student Office and student association offices where students visit most often in their first year.*
Objective 1.2: *Promote through orientation period.*
    Action 1.2.1: *Prepare some slides highlighting the resources for new students. These slides are to be included in the university introduction workshops that are presented to new students in the orientation weeks.*
    Action 1.2.2: *Prepare a bookmark about the Centre and its resources. These bookmarks are to be given away to students in the stands set up for orientation period.*
    Action 1.2.3: *Prepare welcome message for new students. This message is to be sent out in a newsletter to all the new students in the welcome week.*
Strategy 2: *Marketing the Centre through different media.*
Objective 2.1: *Utilize social media tools.*
    Action 2.1.1: *Design customer-centered and inspiring short messages about careers/work. Also, select a few resources focusing on the topics of career exploration and self-assessment.*
    Action 2.1.2: *Post the designed messages and selected resources in rotation on Twitter and Facebook throughout the year.*
    Action 2.1.3: *Prepare 12 reviews on career-related websites/database/books. Each month, post one review on the Centre's blog.*
Objective 2.2: *Utilize the display area in and around the Centre.*
    Action 2.2.1: *Prepare several posters about the Centre and its resources. Post them in rotation on the billboards in the Student Services building.*
    Action 2.2.2: *Prepare a list of career books that are interesting to new students. Display them in rotation in the Centre's book display area.*
    Action 2.2.3: *Prepare a career handout for new students to take home whenever they visit the Centre.*
Objective 2.3: *Utilize the Centre's website.*
    Action 2.3.1: *Expand the existing new-student section on the website by adding a list of resources useful to new students.*
    Action 2.3.2: *Create a career-related FAQ section that links to career resources for new students on the website.*

Wendy O'Brien, Richmond Public Library, Richmond, VA

Marketing Plan for Technology Outreach, Richmond Public Library (RPL)

Target audience. *People who need help with technology who do not have computer or internet access at home.*

Needs of the community that we can fulfill. *Help with online job or benefit applications in an area without local high-speed internet.*

Mission/vision. *To help people improve their quality of life through assistance with employment.*

Desired outcomes. *People will begin to see the RPL as an important community resource.*

Measurement. *Have two attendees at monthly sessions (the RPL currently only has two workstations).*

Actions needed to achieve outcome. *Educate the instructors on current employment application techniques, perhaps partner with local employment office.*

Promotion techniques. *Posters/flyers in neighboring low-income areas and employment office, newspapers.*

Technologies to put in place. *If successful, perhaps purchase additional workstation or offer additional classes to allow for more attendees.*

Carol Munroe, media specialist, Milwaukee, WI

The advantage of working in a school library is that I have, to a certain extent, a captive audience in the students. This means, at the very least, that it becomes much cheaper to market to my population – they're already in the doors. That said, getting them in the door doesn't guarantee keeping them in the door. In addition, to maintain the library's budget and make improvements, I will have to convince the school's administration of the library's value.

- *Space.* For better or worse, a well-designed, inviting space is an essential part of marketing any library. People have to want to be there, after all. I'm starting with a design/furniture budget of not much more than $0 – I open with shelving and some basic trapezoid tables (the kind that can be joined into hexagons). So creating student artwork displays is a logical choice both for my budget and for helping students develop a sense of ownership over the space. This also allows me to collaborate with the art teacher and begin establishing the value of the library in the larger scheme of the school. I will also supplement student art displays with posters from this summer's and past ALA conferences. They may not be exotic, but they can serve as a base until I have more flexibility to improve the space.
- *Social media.* Develop a Facebook page. Ideally, this page will focus on providing news on special events/programs the library will offer and readers' advisory services – particularly encouraging the students to provide recommendations to each other. That buzz can then draw them back to the library.
- *Displays.* Displays can be relatively cheap, making them a good way to grab more attention on a budget – particularly for things already in the public eye like readalikes for popular movies. Goal: two displays that rotate on a staggered monthly basis (a new display every other week), one aligned more to popular culture, the other with a more academic focus.
- *Community involvement.* At a bare minimum, I plan to request and install a comments box to get feedback all year long and conduct a survey at the end of the year. Hopefully, students will feel comfortable leaving honest feedback on the library's Facebook page, but realistically, it may take them a while.
- *Keep track.* I will monitor statistics for circulation (including a special category for display books), programs hosted, attendees for those programs, any special "I love the library/Miss

Carol because _____!" stories, and track resources provided to staff. I have watched the libraries I've worked at before struggle to prove their value, and I know that tracking all those things will be immensely valuable when it comes time to justify the library's worth to the school's administration.

To summarize

- Marketing your library's resources and services is an important aspect for any library that wishes to remain in its current position and to grow and thrive.
- For solo librarians, marketing is imperative – it is the life-blood and the tool to remain a vital and vigorous institution in any setting.
- Solo librarians must use various innovative marketing strategies compatible with their library's holdings, needs, and budgets to enable them to demonstrate that they provide important and necessary services to their organizations and institutions.

References

Barber, Peggy (2014). "Contagious marketing". *American Libraries*, *45*(2), 32–35.

Chan, Christopher (2012). "Marketing the academic library with online social network advertising". *Library Management*, *33*(8/9), 479–489.

Garoufallou, Emmanouel, Siatri, Rania, Zafeiriou, Georgia, and Balampanidou, Ekaterini (2013). "The use of marketing concepts in library services: a literature review". *Library Review*, *62*(4/5), 312–334.

Jose, Antony, and Bhat, Ishwara (2007). "Marketing of library and information services: a strategic perspective". *Journal of Business Perspective*, *11*(2), 23–28.

Kaushik, Anna, and Arora, Jagdish (2012). "Blogs on marketing library services". *DESIDOC Journal of Library & Information Technology*, *32*(2), 186–192.

Merriam-Webster (2011). *Webster's College Dictionary* (11th edn), available at: *www.m-w.com* (accessed: 14 March 2014).

Robinson, Cynthia, K. (2012). "Peter Drucker on marketing: applications and implications for libraries". *The Bottom Line: Managing Library Finances*, *25*(1), 4–12.

Further reading

Alman, Susan, W. (2007). *Crash Course for Marketing in Libraries*. Santa Barbara, CA: Libraries Unlimited/ABC-CLIO.

Barber, Peggy, and Wallace, Linda (2010). *Building a Buzz: Libraries and Word-of-Mouth Marketing*. Chicago, IL: ALA Editions.

Doucett, Elisabeth (2008). *Creating Your Library Brand: Communicating Your Relevance and Value to Your Patrons*. Chicago, IL: ALA Editions.

Professional development

3

The primary and traditional method of librarian professional development has been, and remains, the live conference or annual meeting (Breeding, 2009). Here, librarians learn new materials in classes and network with their fellow professionals after the classes end. Live conferences, of course, are still the main way most librarians learn new skills and meet new people (as well as getting a much-needed break from work!), but technology has changed things, and for the better. The webinar, via the internet, and the podcast, via the internet or other smart device, have allowed librarians the ability to develop as professionals and learn new skills anytime, anyplace, and anywhere. They allow solo librarians, who cannot leave their libraries as easily or as often as their colleagues in larger libraries, to learn at their desks and on the job. A myriad of courses are available online from institutions such as the American Library Association, as well as informal courses available on YouTube and social media sites such as Facebook and Twitter (Breeding, 2009; Stranack, 2012). The major drawback of these wonderful technologies is that the important component of face-to-face meeting and networking does not work as well in the world of the internet and the iPod – true, we have Skype and other types of webcams and software (such as Voicethread) that do allow librarians to make contact in cyberspace and hold a live, face-to-face conversation with other librarians, but a quality of actually meeting and talking to a living human being is lost with webinars and podcasts. So what is the solution for allowing face-to-face contact for busy solo librarians? The first step is the realization that live meetings are important for any librarian's growth as an information professional. If a solo librarian cannot attend classes, why not attend social gatherings for librarians, or create your own social gatherings? Why not volunteer to serve on local, regional, or national committees doing work you are interested in pursuing? Why not get more involved in teaching librarians with learning instructional design skills to create continuing education classes for librarians? The main idea here is to be creative and find ways to maintain professional connections with other librarians, even if you do not work with them. Doing so allows solo librarians not only to meet other librarians but also to learn from them. The tendency for solo librarians is to remain as solo professionals, but with today's technology you should find no excuses to become an important and vital part of the library community and to learn new skills as a solo librarian.

What are the ways to accomplish a richer and more varied professional development? I describe several below.

Meetings and networking

Meetings are a time-honored method of networking and learning from other librarians; there is something positive to be said for meeting others face to face and learning what they do to make their libraries a more open and inviting place for their patrons, no matter who these are. It also helps to leave your library for a while and converse with peers in a relaxing and open setting. Many librarians who work in public and academic libraries consider annual meetings a perk of being a librarian – but many solo librarians cannot leave their libraries as easily as their other colleagues. A new idea that has been developed in the last few years is the personal learning network, or PLN. According to Cathy Jo Nelson (2012), "a PLN can be defined simply as a group of people who interact for the purpose of learning, and who give and take with the goal of sharing, growing, and being an active participant for a greater cause". For solo librarians, given smart phones, Skype, and the internet, a PLN is precisely what they need to network and meet counterparts to further their own greater cause, sharing information and experience of how to manage one-person libraries successfully. What other networking and learning options are open to them?

Webinars and podcasts

Technological advances in the last decade alone have allowed for meetings to be held online – many organizations offer free (or limited-cost) webinars on a vast variety of library topics so that solo librarians can stay current and up to date with all sorts of trends and issues. Library consortia and library schools, as well as library organizations such as the American Library Association, offer many webinars. Podcasting of webinars and other educational events offers even more flexibility for solo librarians to learn at home away from work in their own time schedule. In addition to the ubiquitous YouTube, podcasts can be found on most library association sites, as well as those of library consortia and library schools, and academic and commercial websites.

Some librarians, however, do proclaim the superiority of live events – you are meeting the person, listening to a live lecture, and posing questions to the presenter. This may lose something in a webinar setting, but with the exception of not being present at the lecture, a librarian can participate in a webinar and ask questions just like their live attending counterparts. And the cost of travel and time the librarian is away from work adds to the worth of the use of webinars and podcasts in professional training and development for solo librarians. They are an enhancement of the live lecture, and while they will never replace it, they are a useful and resourceful addition to solo librarians' professional development, given their limitations on time and budget.

Social media and networking

In addition to numerous webinars and podcasts available for skills development, solo librarians can network and make new professional connections with social media: Twitter, Facebook, and LinkedIn are the main sites being used by many people to contact other professionals and learn from them or work with them on projects or other aspects of librarianship and library management. Of these sites, LinkedIn is perhaps the most useful, as solo librarians can chat with other librarians, post a resumé, search for additional projects to work with others, and receive help and assistance with questions they may have. Twitter and Facebook are helpful for just communicating with a vast number of professional contacts, which makes them good sites for this task. Listservs are another convenient and easy way to make contacts with other librarians, learn about various conferences and webinars available, and find out about the latest trends, technologies, and strategies available to solo librarians to enable them to manage their libraries efficiently and effectively.

One caveat should be mentioned about social media and networking: solo librarians should only post, of course, professional information and material that they wish others to see and read, and should become aware of the terms and conditions of each of the social media sites that they choose to utilize for their professional development (these documents are very lengthy, but should be reviewed, as they deal with posted content and who owns that content, for instance). Terms of Service Didn't Read (www.tosdr.org) is an excellent website that provides concise summaries of the main social media sites, such as Twitter and Google, to help solo librarians navigate these important terms and decide which website works best for their needs.

Writing

While not all solo librarians will want (or need) to write a book on their experiences, many of them can gain visibility in the library community by offering to write book or internet reviews for the vast number of library publications, such as *Library Journal*, *School Library Journal*, *Reference and User Services Quarterly*, and *College & Research Library News*. Writing these reviews allows solo librarians to learn skills that will help them as they prepare learning and research materials for their libraries, as well as the aforementioned visibility in the library community. There is nothing quite as gratifying as seeing your name in print and actually assisting other librarians in choosing materials as part of collection development for their libraries. The more ambitious solo librarians can also volunteer to help others, particularly academic librarians, to write a peer-reviewed article on a topic that interests them or about which they have knowledge in researching and writing. A librarian writing, and collaborating with fellow librarians in writing, scholarly articles and books contributes to learning and improving writing skills, as well as increasing and enhancing the visibility of the organization where s/he works. Writing skills can also be used for practical purposes, such as grant applications, which can enable your organization to obtain funds to run a library and library programs beyond a solo librarian's budget.

Teaching

Most solo librarians, as part of their work, make presentations to either patrons or colleagues on various topics in librarianship, from research to reference to management; solo librarians, like most librarians, consider this work bibliographic instruction, and a key part of their profession. They possess the skills to create PowerPoint or Prezi online presentations, as well as to teach the material to their intended audience. Why not take this a step further and teach an online or live class? Many colleges and schools offer adjunct positions in courses such as research and writing skills that most librarians have the knowledge and ability to teach, which can lead to other teaching opportunities. Not only do you assist students in learning valuable skills, but you learn valuable teaching skills as well.

Since April 2011 I have taught, as a national online faculty adjunct, a course in research and report writing at Rasmussen College, a regional college located in the US Midwest. This is an 11-week, upper-level, required course for nearly all the students at the college, with their final grade based on a paper (having learned all the material on researching and writing a paper in the assignments preceding the final paper's submission). In early 2012 the school asked me to teach the same course in an accelerated six-week format that included holding live weekly lectures via a software platform similar to GoToMeeting.com, Wimba, Blackboard, Moodle, or other online instruction software. Many of the students attended these weekly live lectures, and I enjoyed preparing my own PowerPoint presentations and speaking to them on the course material from my own experience as a librarian, researcher, and writer. I continue to teach for the school presently, and I know that my teaching skills make me a better librarian, and vice versa. I am planning to learn instructional design in the future, as I want to become more involved in online learning beyond teaching. What is important here is never to stop learning new skills as a solo librarian; they will not only enrich your life but also enable you to work in new areas and fields that you did not know existed until you found them.

Case studies

Amanda Tarbet, reference librarian, MGH Institute of Health Professions, Boston, MA

Twitter isn't really my thing, but I do follow some great librarians on tumblr. We are all pretty good about posting interesting and informative stuff about librarianship. If you join tumblr, check out the "tumblarians" tag (as well as "libraries" and "librarians") to find and interact with the community. In the past year, I would say that participating has done a lot to make me feel less "alone" in my job.

Back in May [2013], I had the opportunity to go to MLA '13 [Medical Library Association conference] for a day, and this year I have even more money for conference attendance, so I'm looking forward to finding one. I also am aspiring to contribute in some way, whether it is with a paper or a poster. My supervisor and I have made it a goal for the next year. We also are going to try to meet with the librarian at the hospital's patient education library to discuss how are services can complement each other.

Other than that, this is my professional development course for the fiscal year that is about to end. We are encouraged to take at least one a year. I tried looking for other continuing education services like Simmons, but could not really find any. And because one of my goals for the next year is to do more instruction, I'm currently gathering as many resources as I can on the topic because I want to improve my skills with both presenting and designing sessions. It helps that I am only part time and have extra time to research stuff on my own.

I also recommend lynda.com as a great training resource, especially for software. I learned programs like Adobe Illustrator and Captivate using the site, and I just love it. It's $25/month or $250 for a year, and they are offering a seven-day trial right now. If it's out of your budget, there are also tutorials on YouTube for just about every software you would need to use – it just requires some searching to find the good ones.

Elyse Seltzer, librarian, Shore Country Day School, Beverly, MA

I try to do as much professional development as I can. I definitely used more than my share last year, but they said that I could since it was my first year at the school, so I haven't done as much this year. I always go to the Massachusetts School Library Association fall conference and try to incorporate at least one thing that I see there. I used to go to events with the Foundation for Children's Books. I subscribe to the MSLA listserv and Booklinks, *School Library Journal*, *Horn Book Magazine*, Booklist, and Library Sparks which is great for lesson and display ideas. I like to go to assorted events where I can see authors speak. I hope to bring an author to the school every year but I would prefer to know what I am getting. So someone said they wanted Ashley Bryan to come, so I went to a colloquy for Children's Literature New England since I knew Ashley Bryan would be there. I am a member of the Independent School Librarians Association (EISLA), and we meet about twice a year.

Also when I got hired they were nervous since I was right out of school, so they said that I could go back to the school where I was an intern twice and then they would come to me twice. So I have a mentor librarian even though I am not part of a district. It's great because I have individuals who I know I could directly call or email with particular problems or questions.

I also do professional development that connects more to the teacher part of me. My school is a part of the National Association for Independent Schools and every year any person of color who wants can be sent to the People of [Color] Conference or they can go to the White Privilege conference if they prefer.

Martha Kennedy, librarian, Concord Academy, Concord, MA

My school is quite supportive of professional development programs. Last summer I had my second "summer sabbatical". This basically meant I was awarded a grant to travel and focus on some aspect of library renewal, etc. My first summer grant (2003) allowed me to attend the two-week Oxbridge program on "The Library and the Academy". It was terrific and I highly recommend it. This past summer, I traveled to Cambodia on the first-ever Where There Be Dragons Educator's Program. I know all about how wonderful Dragon trips are for students as I am the go-to person for summer programs. When this opportunity opened up for me, I took it. We went all over Cambodia and visited many libraries – from small primary schools to a brand-new university library built with funding from the government of Thailand. The focus of the entire program was NGOs [non-governmental organizations] and their effectiveness in rebuilding challenged parts of the world. After Haiti, Cambodia is the host to the second-greatest number of NGOs on the planet. This summer, I plan to connect with the local Cambodian community in the nearby city of Lowell.

During the year, I attend four meetings sponsored by the Greater Boston Cooperative Library Association (CLA), a group of 60+ independent school libraries. The CLA awards up to three grants each year and recipients are required to provide a program in the year following the award. I'm about to step down as treasurer and membership secretary after five years. This course and a second Simmons online course will round out my professional development for this year. When I emailed my dean of faculty about this class during March break, he promptly replied in the affirmative. I always have good intentions about heading to an ALA meeting – Washington, DC was nearly in the plans for last summer, but the bigger trip won out.

One thing to prioritize is that despite your being *the* librarian at your institution, it is important that you take time to attend a few big meetings. Ask and you might be pleasantly surprised that your district, department, or supervisor will support you. Also realize that many state library organizations provide grants for new librarians or small libraries to allow staff to attend such events. Think about ways to connect with other folks who serve as librarians at like institutions.

Lisa Lin, career resource consultant, McGill University Career Planning Service, Montreal, Quebec, Canada

My professional development activities are more passive. What I do to keep myself updated, so far, is:

- read some library-related materials (e.g. *Computers in Libraries* and Special Library's listserv)
- participate in local library conferences, if money allows
- as of this year, I started taking a few online courses to keep up my skills.

Other than that, I do volunteer work in a local church. I teach children's Sunday school. I come up with my own curriculum for kids and prepare all the materials by myself. A good thing about this is that it helps me to be creative in finding solutions with low costs (materials can be expensive…). Also, it enhances my ability to instruct others.

To summarize

- Professional development is an important part of a librarian's growth and progress as an information specialist.

- New technologies exist to allow solo librarians to meet, to network, and to share experiences and resources to allow them to learn from their peers.
- Teaching and writing allow solo librarians to learn new skills that will enable them to become more effective information specialists.

References

Breeding, Marshall (2009). "Social networking strategies for professionals". *The Systems Librarian*, *9*, 29–31.

Nelson, Cathy Jo (2012). "RIF or VIP? Having a PLN can help". *Knowledge Quest*, *41*(2), 70–73.

Stranack, Kevin (2012). "The connected librarian: using social media for 'do it yourself' professional development". *Canadian Journal of Library and Information Practice and Research*, *7*(1), 1–5.

Further reading

Keiser, Barbie E. (2012). "Professional development and continuing education". *Online*, *36*(3), 20–27.

Collection development

4

How does a solo librarian learn collection development skills?

Many years ago, when I was a library school student, I wanted to enroll in a collection development course, as I believed it was essential to know these skills to become a successful librarian (and the subject interested me as well). Unfortunately, I could not take the course, as I could not rearrange my schedule to accommodate it. A few weeks later, I asked one of my colleagues enrolled in the course what she thought of it; she said that the instructor read entirely from the book and did not provide any additional useful information. I went on, in my library career, to ensure that I learned good collection development skills on my own, and I am proud to say that learning this way proved far more helpful and useful to me than sitting in a classroom to learn about collection development.

This is not to criticize any collection development instructors in graduate library programs or to devalue books on collection development, but I have found that learning collection development on one's own may be preferable for librarians, especially solo librarians. Why is this so? Book knowledge can take one only so far, and there are numerous and well-written texts for librarians to read; solo librarians have to become actively involved in collection development, as no one else in their libraries can do so, so learning on your own from experience in working with developing your library's collection is a great motivator to acquire the skills to create a collection that will be utilized. I would, of course, supplement this on-the-job learning with a few texts, a few webinars, and, most importantly, discussion with colleagues on this topic (both in cyberspace and in person). Learning by doing does not take place in a vacuum; learning involves active participation with one's peers to find out what a solo librarian is doing correctly (and incorrectly) in collection development.

What constitute good collection development skills?

There is not one definite set of written rules that constitute good and effective collection development skills for all librarians. I have found that for solo librarians, creating an official written library policy for collection development is very useful and helpful; it will eliminate, after a good deal of trial and error, an official policy about how to proceed (of course, this policy should be updated regularly – I would recommend reviewing it every quarter or six months to include any updates on policy and remove outdated or changed policies). The policy does not have to be lengthy – one or two pages should be more than adequate – but it should be understood by anyone who reads it, not just librarians, and should be concise and to the point. Many solo librarians have management that need to realize the importance of good collection development skills, and a solid, succinct policy will not only help them understand what constitutes good collection development, but will help solo librarians communicate to them the importance of a well-developed library (perhaps, but not always, resulting in sufficient purchasing budgets!).

What materials do solo librarians include in their collection development?

In the past, library collection development generally primarily involved books, both reference and circulating material. Today, of course, most libraries are hybrid, having both print and electronic resources. Collection development depends on what solo librarians are responsible for creating – most handle the book purchases, and some handle the electronic database purchases. This depends on their management responsibilities, which vary from library to library.

Regarding print, solo librarians need to create a collection development policy to determine how much money they have to spend on purchases, and also what subject matter needs purchasing, the currency of the materials, the relevancy of the materials to their collection, and other parameters. Solo librarians should solicit advice and ideas from their patrons, faculty, and students, usually through the use of quarterly surveys (which can be paper-based or electronic; electronic-based are more convenient, as they are easier to refer to and to organize for purchase histories). A solo librarian should have knowledge of his/her collection's content, but may not have the same amount of knowledge when it comes to adding new material to the collection. This is where librarians should take advantage of their users' knowledge on what to add to the library's purchases to make it an even more resource-rich collection. Doing so also helps solo librarians communicate effectively with their users; satisfied users make for continual users of a library.

With regard to choosing electronic databases, many solo librarians have a library director or manager (possibly an IT manager as well) who prepares a budget and determines what purchases will be made and when. However, some solo librarians, given the size of their libraries, do their own budgeting and determination for electronic databases. Here, a solo librarian needs to work, with management and users, in more detail and depth than with print material, as electronic databases can consume a great deal of a library budget. Solo librarians should make all efforts to communicate with their users, as well as seek advice (on library listservs, for instance) on how to purchase electronic databases that will function effectively as part of their library's collection.

Tips and techniques on purchasing items at a lower cost

Many solo librarians are not fortunate enough to have a large budget to purchase books; but with a bit of ingenuity, librarians can find ways to purchase items at little or no cost to them.

In the past, I worked closely with several publishing houses which sold us textbooks. I asked them, given their business with our school, could they donate several books that would be useful ancillary texts for the students to use in the library that were not, of course, teacher editions, answer keys, or workbooks. Most of the publishers gladly complied, and I was able to build a solid collection based on my good relationships with these publishers and with our continued purchases of textbooks.

Another good source of inexpensive books for your library's collection is a book jobber. A book jobber usually sells books at a discount rate for educational institutions, and may also catalog and include other processing in the business transaction. I purchased books for many years from a jobber that was similar to a large bookstore, with books lying on pallets for easy display. By using a book jobber, I increased my book collection size a great deal – and with the rise of the internet, many of these jobbers now appear online, making the cost even less than working from a free-standing store or warehouse.

I would also look into online purchases from the usual suspects, such as Amazon. com, or other sources, such as public library sales or other estate sales. You never know what you may find, and although you will have to catalog your material, purchasing at a bargain price greatly outweighs the inconvenience of doing so.

Finally, consider the novel approach of sharing your collection with another related library or public library – you would have access to their materials, as they would to yours. Not only does this improve relations between libraries, but patrons of both libraries win with greater and expanded access to both collections. In one of my solo positions, I made an agreement with the local public library to share certain resources and allow its patrons to use some of our material. Doing so did help us elevate our profile in the community as a resource that could be used when people needed information that may not be available at the public library. You may want to create an agreement to deal with particular sharing parameters or material damages, for instance, but an agreement is worth having to expand the size of your collection for your users.

Collection development may be a daunting task for solo librarians, but with skill and a bit of thinking and ingenuity, it can result in creating a truly resourceful library.

Case studies

These case studies, from my former students now at different libraries, include such specific policies as collection development parameters and weeding materials.

Lisa Lin, career resource consultant, McGill University Career Planning Service, Montreal, Quebec, Canada

Change Issue/Project: Building an E-Book Collection

Projected time: Six months besides the regular tasks.
Goal 1: The feasibility assessment can start in the end of winter semester (April–June).

Goal 2: The implementation is recommended to be in summer when it is low season (July–August).
Goal 3: The collection of data should be during the peak period (September) and the evaluation of the project should be after the busy period (October–November).

Goal 1: Feasibility assessment

Aim: To assess what resources are needed for this project.
Projected time: Three months.
Objective 1.1: Determine resources needed to build an e-book collection.
  Action 1.1.1: Assess the library's current resources including technology, infrastructure, device compatibility, human resources, time, start-up, and ongoing costs for this project.
  Action 1.1.2: Review the current collection development policy and the scope of the project.
Objective 1.2: Collect the features of how to build and manage an e-book collection.
  Action 1.2.1: Contact local libraries that already have an e-book collection for suggestions and best practices.
  Action 1.2.2: Research different business models and steps to build an e-book collection.
  Action 1.2.3: Analyze the impact of business models on current collection, library policy, licensing, and the system.
Objective 1.3: Communicate the idea to gain internal support.
  Action 1.3.1: Identify main stakeholders, the benefits of having an e-book collection for each stakeholder, and training needed.
  Action 1.3.2: Write up a report detailing the cost-benefit and steps involved in building an e-book collection.
  Action 1.3.3: Prepare slides to present in staff meeting, collect feedback, and adjust the plan accordingly.

Goal 2: Building an e-book collection

Aim: To select and set up the best e-book platform in the library.
Projected time: Two months.
Objective 2.1: Evaluate and select an e-book platform.
Note: Control over expenditure is a big issue in this library, and the minimization of the change of acquisitions and circulation structures is desired. Therefore, only third-party platforms with web-hosted option and large e-book display devices are considered.
  Action 2.1.1: Establish e-book selection factors, and set up approval plans for e-books.
  Action 2.1.2: Identify and request trials for an e-book collection from potential third-party platform providers.
  Action 2.1.3: Review licensing issues and determine the best user access model for the library.
  Action 2.1.4: Put together the results of the review and share in staff meeting for input.
  Action 2.1.5: Evaluate and select the best e-book platform for the library.

Objective 2.2: Set up the selected e-book collection.
> Note: The library's OPAC is developed in-house and manual entry is required. Therefore, the e-book cataloging is not considered in this outline.
> Action 2.2.1: Identify and collect potential e-book vendor information.
> Action 2.2.2: Purchase e-books (title-by-title acquisition) according to collection policy.
> Action 2.2.3: Provide training to the front-end staff to answer e-book-related questions.
> Action 2.3.4: Prepare, with help from front-end staff, a guide and an e-book circulation policy for patrons.

Objective 2.3: Promote and increase visibility of e-book collection.
> Action 2.3.1: Inform other university career centers about the e-book collection.
> Action 2.3.2: Form a marketing committee to integrate e-book promotion into the overall marketing plan.

Goal 3: Evaluating e-book collection performance

Aim: To assess and evaluate the e-book collection and collect feedback to better serve patrons in the future.
Projected time: One month. Evaluation should be conducted the first month after the implementation and every six months afterwards.
Objective 3.1: Review e-book adoption.
> Action 3.1.1: With staff members, determine methods of assessment (usage, survey, etc.) for the e-book collection.
> Action 3.1.2: Collect data using the determined assessment methods.
> Action 3.1.3: Group impact factors from the results and create a report for staff members for feedback.
> Action 3.1.4: Solve challenges found from the assessment and feedback.

Objective 3.2: Document e-book adoption.
> Action 3.2.1: Write up documentation of the e-book implementation process.
> Action 3.2.1: Archive any project-relevant files for future reference.

Wendy O'Brien, Richmond Public Library, Richmond, VA

Materials Selection Policy

Approved by the Library Board of Trustees, 13 February, 2010

I. Objectives

The Richmond Public Library acquires and makes available materials which inform, educate, entertain, and enrich people's lives. Since it is not possible for any library to acquire all materials, it is necessary to employ a policy of selectivity in acquisitions. The Library provides, within its financial limitations, a collection of reliable materials embracing broad areas of knowledge. Included are works of enduring value as well as timely materials on current bestseller lists. Within the framework of these broad objectives, selection is based on community needs, from those expressed and those from community demographics and evidence of areas of interest. Our current population structure in Richmond from the 2000 census is as follows: 31.1% children and young adults; 47.5% adults; and 21.4% senior citizens. Allocation of the materials budget will also be determined by usage indicators, and objectives for development of the collection. Our usage statistics from 2009 show the following: adult fiction, 22%; Videos and DVDs, 20%; children's picture books, 16%; juvenile fiction, 10%; with the remaining 40% spread among various departments.

New formats shall be considered for the collection, when industry reports and evidence from local requests show that a significant portion of the community population has the necessary technology to make use of the format. Availability of the format, the cost per item, and the Library's ability to acquire and handle the items will also be factors in determining when a format will be collected. Similar considerations will influence the decision to delete a format from the Library's collection.

It is the Library's goal to provide the Richmond community with library materials that reflect a wide range of views, expressions, opinions, and interests. Specific acquisitions may include items that may be unorthodox or unpopular with the majority or controversial in nature. The Library's acquisition of these items does not constitute endorsement of their content but rather makes available their expression.

The Library provides free access to materials in a number of formats (print, media, and electronic) to all patrons. Library users make their own choices as to what they will use based on individual interests and concerns. The Richmond Public Library supports the right of each family to decide which items are appropriate for use by their children. Responsibility for a child's use of library materials lies with his or her parent or guardian. The Richmond Public Library adheres to the principles of intellectual freedom adopted by the American Library Association, as expressed in the Library Bill of Rights and the Freedom to View Statements. The Richmond Public Library subscribes to the Freedom to Read statement prepared by the American Library Association and the Association of American Publishers.

II. Criteria for selection

General criteria for selecting library materials are listed below. An item need not meet all of the criteria in order to be acceptable.

- The need for added material in subject areas.
- Availability of material through interlibrary loan.
- Physical limitation of the library building.
- Relevance to community needs.
- Budgetary considerations.
- Public demand, interest, or need.
- Contemporary significance, popular interest, or permanent value.
- Prominence, authority, and/or competence of author, creator, or publisher.
- Timeliness of material.
- Relation to existing collections.
- Statement of challenging, original, or alternative point of view.

- Authenticity of historical, regional, or social setting.
- The special needs of library patrons for materials in accessible formats.

Each type of material must be considered in terms of its own merit and the audience for whom it is intended. No single standard can be applied in all cases. Some materials may be judged primarily in terms of artistic merit, scholarship, or value to humanity; others are selected to satisfy the informational, recreational, or educational interests of the community.

While the Library works closely with the education program within the area's education facilities, the Library does not have resources to add textbooks to the collection.

All librarians have a professional responsibility to be inclusive, not exclusive, in developing collections. Efforts will be made to provide materials representing all viewpoints.

Tools used in selection include professional journals, publishers' promotional materials, and reviews from reputable sources. Purchase suggestions from library patrons are welcome and are given serious consideration.

III. Responsibility for selection

Selection of all materials shall be the responsibility of the professional librarian who operates within the framework of policies determined by the Library Board of Trustees, and based on the criteria cited above.

IV. Collection maintenance, replacement, and weeding

The librarian regularly reviews items in the collection to ensure that they continue to meet patrons' needs. Materials that are worn, obsolete, unused, old editions, or unnecessarily duplicated are removed. It is the responsibility of the librarian to assess the need for replacing materials that are damaged, destroyed, or lost. Items are not automatically replaced. Decisions are based on need, demand, budget, and criteria for selection.

V. Gifts

The Richmond Public Library accepts gifts of new or gently used books, DVDs, videos, and music or books on CD. Gifts shall meet the same collection criteria as purchased materials. The Library retains unconditional ownership of all donations and makes the final decision on acceptance, use, or disposition. The appraisal of the gift for tax purposes is the responsibility of the donor.

When the Library receives a cash gift for the purchase of materials, whether as a memorial or for any other purpose, the general nature or subject area of the materials to be purchased will be based upon the wishes of the donor. The librarian in accordance with the needs and selection policies of the Library will make selection of specific titles.

Special collections and memorial collections will not be shelved as separate physical entities. Such collections will be accepted only with the understanding that they will be integrated into the general collections.

VI. Reconsideration of library materials

The Library recognizes that some materials are controversial and that any given item may offend some patrons. Selection of materials will not be made on the basis of anticipated approval or disapproval but solely on the basis of the objectives set forth in this policy. Library materials will not be marked or identified to show approval or disapproval of their contents, and no library materials will be sequestered.

While a person may reject materials for himself or herself and for his or her children, he or she cannot exercise censorship to restrict access to the materials by others. Patrons requesting that an item be removed, relocated, labeled, and/or restricted from the collection may complete a reconsideration of library materials form.

VII. Procedures for request for reconsideration

Any individual expressing an objection or concern about library material should receive respectful attention from the staff member first approached. The following steps will be used when dealing with an individual requesting an item to be reconsidered.

- A request for reconsideration form should be obtained from the Library and filled out by the complainant. Use one form per item.
- The first step is meeting with the librarian who is responsible for the collection.
- If agreement is not reached in the first step, then the complainant is referred to the Library Board.
- The Library Board's decision is final.

VIII. Previous reconsideration requests

Requests to reconsider materials which have previously undergone the reconsideration process will be referred to the Librarian. Repeated or redundant requests by an individual or a group to reconsider materials with a differing title but similar content will be restricted as follows: if the Librarian concludes a request may be redundant, he/she will notify the complainant/complainants that the item(s) in question, having already undergone a thorough review and reconsideration process, will not be reevaluated.

In the event that a complainant charges a particular item is not protected under the First Amendment of the Constitution of the United States of America, the onus of proof rests with the complainant.

Amanda Target, reference librarian, MGH Institute of Health Professions, Boston, MA

The MGH IHP Community Health Collection, 2013

Introduction

About the collection

The IHP Community Health Collection was founded in 2012 with materials inherited from a previous Massachusetts Prevention Resource Center. As of 2013, it has over 1,300 items including 837 monographs, 246 curricula, 86 kits, 67 DVDs/ videos, and 130 visual aids.

Location

Building 36, 4th Floor
MGH Institute of Health Professions
Charlestown Navy Yard
36 First Avenue
Boston, MA 02129

Policy purpose and audience

This policy is intended to be used by library staff as a set of guidelines for selection of new materials and evaluation of current materials in the Community Health Collection. It will also inform users, stakeholders, and community members of the selection criteria used to develop the library's holdings, as well as what resources they may expect to find and why. This policy is supplemental to the IHP Library collection development policy. It will be reviewed annually and revised as needed.

Users

The library's primary users are the students, faculty, and staff of the Institute. Additional users include affiliates from Massachusetts General Hospital, Partners Healthcare, the Charlestown community, and the greater Boston community. The collection is open to the public, with borrowing privileges granted to Massachusetts residents. The majority of users external to the Institute will be community health educators and nurses.

Programs served

The library supports a specific class within the IHP School of Nursing, "NS 521 Community Nursing Principles and Theories", in which nursing students are introduced to the care of families and aggregate populations as clients within the community. Principles and theories of family and community health are discussed in relation to the application of nursing process. Students examine the influence of social, political, economic, and physical forces on the health status and health needs of families and community aggregate populations. Students participate in a community health promotion activity with families and aggregates, integrating theories and principles of epidemiology, program planning, and health behavior change.

Selection Criteria

Current focus
The current focus of the collection is on Community Health, which combines aspects of nursing, public health, human anatomy and physiology, education, ethics,

psychology, and more. Emphasis is on recently published materials, however some
resource types (e.g. anatomical models) are not dependent on publication year
for their value. Generally geographic origin is not considered when evaluating
materials, with the exception of resources specific to the state of Massachusetts,
which may be collected more comprehensively.

Resource types and formats

A variety of resource types will be collected by the library, including monographs
and school curricula material in print and electronic formats; audiovisual materials;
two-dimensional visual resources such as posters; and three-dimensional realia such
as anatomical models and multimodal kits. The library also collects resources in the
form of student submissions from the NS 521 class. Materials will be collected at all
reading levels, including juvenile resources. The library will not collect textbooks.

Languages

Materials will primarily be collected in English, but additional languages will be
supported, including (but not limited to) Spanish, French, Chinese, Portuguese, and
Vietnamese. These are the most commonly spoken languages in Boston other than
English according to 2010 census data found in the 2012–2013 *Health of Boston*
report from the Boston Public Health Commission. The terms Spanish, French, and
Portuguese all include use of associated Creole languages.

Gifts in kind

To be determined.

Limitations

Due to our relationship with the Treadwell Library at the Massachusetts General
Hospital, the IHP Community Health Library will not collect materials that are
available through Treadwell, unless specific materials are considered vital for the
use of patrons who do not have access to Treadwell's resources.

Collection Profile

Depth

All materials are collected at a depth of level 2 (Basic Information Level) as defined
by the International Federation of Library Associations and Institutions Section on
Acquisition and Collection Development. Collections that serve to introduce and
define a subject, to indicate the varieties of information available elsewhere, and
to support the needs of general library users through the first two years of college
instruction include:

- a limited collection of monographs and reference works
- a limited collection of representative general periodicals

- defined access to a limited collection of owned or remotely accessed electronic bibliographic tools, texts, datasets, journals, etc.

The collection should be frequently and systematically reviewed for currency of information. Superseded editions and titles containing outdated information should be withdrawn. Classic or standard retrospective materials may be retained.

Subjects

The Community Health Collection uses a unique classification system based on topics in community health and disease prevention.

Collection Evaluation Methods

The size of the collection is small enough that the collection can be evaluated on a resource-by-resource basis. This may change in the future and updates to the policy will reflect that change. The librarians will use a number of quantitative and qualitative indicators to evaluate and, if necessary, weed the collection. Those measures include:

- circulation statistics
- age of materials
- overall inventory
- user feedback and suggestions
- condition of materials
- professional judgment.

Evaluation will ideally be done once a year, with an emphasis on discarding extraneous materials and identifying coverage gaps.

Discards

Any resources removed from the collection may be donated if an appropriate recipient is identified. Other options for discards include a library giveaway/sale, or disposal.

Bibliography

1. *MGH Institute of Health Professions Course Catalog 2012–2013.* Available at: http://mghihp.smartcatalogiq.com/20122013/catalog.
2. Boston Public Health Commission. *Health of Boston 2012–2013.* Available at: www.bphc.org/about/research/Pages/HOB20122013.aspx.
3. International Federation of Library Associations and Institutions: Section on Acquisition and Collection Development (2001) *Guidelines for collection development policy using the conspectus model.* Available at: www.ifla.org/publications/guidelinesforacollectiondevelopmentpolicyusingtheconspectusmodel.

Martha Kennedy, librarian, Concord Academy, Concord, MA

Guidelines for the Selection of Materials – J. Josephine Tucker Library

Responsibility for selection

The Library Director is delegated with the major responsibility for the evaluation, selection, and acquisition of materials for the library. It is the responsibility of the Library Director to work cooperatively with the faculty and solicit their recommendations for materials to be included in the collection. Students and parents are encouraged to make suggestions, and their recommendations will be given consideration in the overall selection process.

In the selection of these materials, the Library Director subscribes to the American Library Association (ALA) Code of Ethics, 1995.

- We provide the highest level of service to all library users through appropriate and useful organized resources; equitable service policies; equitable access; and accurate, unbiased, and courteous responses to all requests.
- We uphold the principles of intellectual freedom and resist all efforts to censor library resources.
- We protect each library user's right to privacy and confidentiality with respect to information sought or received and resources consulted, borrowed, acquired, or transmitted.
- We recognize and respect intellectual property rights.
- We treat co-workers and other colleagues with respect, fairness, and good faith, and advocate conditions of employment that safeguard the rights and welfare of all employees of our institutions.
- We do not advance private interests at the expense of library users, colleagues, or our employing institutions.
- We distinguish between our personal convictions and professional duties and do not allow our personal beliefs to interfere with fair representation of the aims of our institutions or the provision of access to their information resources.
- We strive for excellence in the profession by maintaining and enhancing our own knowledge and skills, by encouraging the professional development of co-workers, and by fostering the aspirations of potential members of the profession.

Objectives of selection

The primary objective for selecting library materials is to implement the academic goals of Concord Academy and to support and enrich the academic life of its students. In addition, these materials should contribute to the development of critical reading skills, literary tastes, and the social and intellectual values of the students. The Library Director seeks to accomplish these goals by the wise selection of materials.

The objective will be achieved through the following:

- educational materials that adequately reflect a pluralistic society;
- a wide range of materials on suitable levels of difficulty with diverse appeal and differing points of view;

- a variety of selections to satisfy the personal and recreational needs of the students enrolled at Concord Academy;
- a positive contribution to the development and mastery of subject area skills and aesthetic taste and judgment; and
- assisting students in the process of developing their social, intellectual, and cultural values.

These materials will:

- implement, support, and be compatible with the academic goals of Concord Academy and the objectives of the individual curricular offerings;
- be selected for a reason and a purpose – materials will be evaluated as to their aesthetic, literary, and social value, appropriateness to student age and general emotional maturity, and relevance to the curriculum;
- reflect a sensitivity to the achievement, needs, and rights of men and women, all ethnicities, and other cultures without stereotype or bias;
- be directed toward maintaining a balance representing various views on political theories and ideologies, religion, public issues, and controversial topics; and
- be judged as a whole, taking into account the author's intent rather than focusing solely upon individual words, phrases, graphics, or incidents taken out of context.

Selection tools

The Library Director shall consult reputable, unbiased, and professionally prepared selection tools such as ALA's *Booklist*, *New York Times Book Review*, and ALA collection development guides to determine which materials are best suited for the collection. Selection is an ongoing process and shall include the discarding of materials no longer relevant and the replacement of lost, worn, or damaged materials still of educational value.

Challenged materials
A procedure shall exist for the challenging or criticism of material(s) by any Concord Academy student, parent, or community member.

- Criticism of any library material (book, periodical, sound recording, etc.) is first to be discussed with the Library Director.
- Criticism of any library material must be submitted in writing, on a complaint form, to the Library Director. Challenged material will remain in use until a decision is rendered. The submitted complaint form will be reviewed in a timely manner.
- A review committee consisting of the department heads, Director of Studies, Dean of Students, Head of School, and parent(s) with expertise in the content area shall confer on challenged materials.
- If upon evaluation of the material the respective committee concludes the complaint is justified, the material will be withdrawn and the complainant so notified. The submitted complaint form will remain on file.

- If upon evaluation of the material the committee concludes that the complaint is not justified, the complainant will be so informed and may submit the criticism in writing to the Head of School within ten school days.
- Allegations thus submitted will be considered by a committee appointed by the Head of School; the committee members shall have expertise in the discipline related to the challenged materials.
- The said committee shall judge the materials based on the objectives and criteria stated herein.
- The committee shall report its recommendations in writing to the Head of School.
- The Head of School shall report his/her decision to the committee, Library Director, parent(s), and the complainant(s).

To summarize

- Collection development is one of the more important skills solo librarians need to learn, as they are the ones responsible for the creation and maintenance of their library's resources.
- Solo librarians need to use all available resources at their disposal, and to be creative in obtaining resources on a limited budget.
- Solo librarians need to work with other librarians and in their communities to give access to resources they may not have available in their own libraries, not only to provide their patrons with research materials, but also to foster a sense of community and participation outside their libraries.

Further reading

Disher, Wayne (2007). *Crash Course in Collection Development*. Santa Barbara, CA: Libraries Unlimited/ABC-CLIO.

Hibner, Holly, and Kelly, Mary (2010). *Making a Collection Count: A Holistic Approach to Library Collection Management*. New York: Neal-Schuman.

Hysell, Shannon Graff (2009). *Recommended Reference Books for Small- and Medium-Sized School Libraries and Media Centers* (Vol. 29). Santa Barbara, CA: Libraries Unlimited/ABC-CLIO.

Johnson, Peggy (2009). *Fundamentals of Collection Development and Management* (2nd edn). Chicago, IL: ALA Editions.

IT resources, troubleshooting, internet security, and library security 5

IT resources and troubleshooting

Computers and printers (and also faxes and scanners) are an integral part of libraries today – in fact, many patrons and students expect them to be ready when they need them (and when they don't need them!). Large libraries usually have an IT professional standing by in case of any emergencies. But the solo librarian is usually himself or herself the IT professional. How does the solo librarian become (somewhat) computer proficient to keep them running smoothly? Here are some suggestions and strategies.

- Learn as much as you can about how a computer and its network operate – this includes the computer hardware and software. For software, most librarians should be knowledgeable about Microsoft Word, Excel, and PowerPoint, as many patrons use these on a regular basis. Java and Linux, for now, can be left to the experts (or referred to in a book or on a website; internet resources for these areas are provided here for your reference). But having at least a rudimentary background in how the major software systems function is always a good idea. This is also true nowadays with smart phones, Kindles, and other handheld devices; at the very least, the solo librarian needs to have information on hand in the library to assist patrons with using these devices, or should be able to direct them to websites that can help them with their questions.
- Creating a book collection devoted to basic computer operating systems (again, hardware and software) will help you and your patrons develop computer literacy. One good starting point is the Teach Yourself Visually book series, published by Wiley (www.wiley.com/compbooks). They are full of easy-to-read text and colorful pictures that any computerphobe will learn to love! When I managed a one-person library, I became very good friends with our textbook publisher (and several other computer book publishers) and, given our textbook spending and budgets with them, I asked for several copies of computer books, telling them that the students and faculty would need to use them as library resources. I built a very comprehensive collection because of my networks and connections. If you don't deal with textbook publishers, I find it cannot hurt to ask them if they have older copies of books that they would not mind parting with to help you build a collection of computer books.
- Nowadays, with e-book databases out of the reach of most solo librarians' budgets, you should compile a list of internet resources dealing with computers and information technology that your patrons (and you) can use to understand more about how computers work. Obviously, given how fast technology changes, you should update this list frequently and stay ahead of the information curve by being current about the latest IT and trends.
- Join a listserv or computer users' group for educational (and moral) support. Not only is this a good way to network with fellow librarians, who can answer any technological questions you may have, but this technology allows solo librarians to meet other librarians and learn (and find help) without leaving their libraries.
- Computer software can be a major expense for a library, as its proprietary nature and copyright can drain any library's budget. Most libraries do require some form of the Microsoft Office suite (which includes Word, PowerPoint, Excel, and Outlook), which may be too prohibitive

in cost to add to library computers, but there are open-source alternatives, such as Apache's Open Office. Created over 20 years ago, this suite of office software contains Writer (similar to Microsoft Word and word processing), Impress (for presentations), Calc (for spreadsheets), and Base (for database development and management). The same applies to email, if Microsoft is too expensive for libraries to obtain. The most recognizable open-source email system is Gmail; another is Mozilla Thunderbird, which is free and can operate on Windows and Mac platforms. eMClient is a third open-source email software that can easily synchronize with Gmail, so this may be preferred by solo librarians who use Gmail, as well as other Google software programs. Finally, those using the Windows 7 or 8 operating systems can use Windows Live Mail for free as an email platform as well (unfortunately, Windows Live Mail is not compatible with the Windows XP operating system). Open-source software gives solo librarians the ability to add the software their libraries need without breaking their operating budgets.

- Take a basic computer class. When I was in library school, I took a computer course (now probably required of all students) – not only did I learn how a computer functions, but I actually took apart an old computer and saw how it works (it was an eye-opening experience, to say the least). Taking such a course (or even dismantling an old computer on your own) may be just the catalyst to become more computer proficient as a solo librarian.
- Another way solo librarians can become more computer literate and troubleshoot computer problems more effectively is to earn a certification (A+ certification, which covers most of how a computer operates and functions, is the best one to obtain). If a solo librarian does not have any IT professionals on staff or on call, a certification can be a life-saver when computer problems arise (and they always do).
- Network and use some savvy. Do you know of a student or a reliable patron who is computer proficient? If so, appeal to their better instincts (or, in the case of students, offer a little money, if available) either to teach you the basics of computer troubleshooting or offer you a few hours of their services to help you maintain the computer equipment (or be available to answer questions by telephone or email, for instance). Figure 5.1

Figure 5.1 Laptop – meet your fellow librarian

Internet security

When your patrons use your library computers, I would safely bet that they are primarily using them for the internet, whether to check their emails, do library research, or conduct other unmentionable activities (which, of course, need to be monitored and curtailed – but that is another course in itself!). Internet security, to ensure that your computers are running properly, is just as important as learning computer troubleshooting skills. One caveat here is that there are many resources, but perhaps a good investment is to review these with an IT professional to ensure that your computers are receiving the best bang for your buck and being protected properly. If an IT professional's services are not within your library's budget, you could find a computer science student who would be willing to assess your computer security situation, or perhaps if you employ or know of a computer science instructor, he or she would be willing to help for a nominal fee.

And another good idea is to create a computer policy for your patrons; at least you will have something on paper to refer to and some order can come out of chaos so that patrons can use your computers in the proper way without ruining them. This is especially important for public libraries and school media centers, as they are public institutions and need to provide guidelines for their users as part of regulations that govern these organizations. Like any policy, computer and internet use policies should be reviewed and potentially updated periodically (e.g. quarterly) to ensure that they remain current with changing computer software.

How does a solo librarian decide what internet security software to purchase, absent any recommendations from an IT professional? Cost and coverage are two areas that are important in choosing the proper software, and there are many free versions of anti-virus, malware, and other internet security software available, such as Avira, Glary Utilities, and Ad-Aware; others, such as AGV, are free for an initial period of time and then available at cost. Internet security software needs to be updated often, as its content changes regularly (given the number of new computer viruses and malware present), so solo librarians need to become knowledgeable about updates in internet security products by reading such trade publications as *PC Magazine* and *Computerworld*, as they contain reviews of new and existing security software.

With a little resourcefulness and motivation, the solo librarian can wear many hats, one those hats being that of an IT expert!

Library security

A library should be a safe and secure place where users can work and conduct research without any concerns for their personal safety and security, as is the case with any public space. This is especially a concern for solo librarians, who cannot rely on a large staff (or a security or police force, in the case of large academic and public libraries) to maintain order and safety. What solo librarians can do to maintain their libraries' safety and security is to create and implement plans and strategies so that their individual spaces are safe. These policies should reflect the library's layout and location in the organization or institution, and should allow for the maximum safety and security for its users (as well as the maximum freedom of users to enter, exit, and use the library without distractions); the plans and policies should be revised regularly, along with the organization's management, to ensure that they remain current and up to date.

The next concern that may arise is implementing safety gates and other electronic tools to provide library security (this is also the case for securing books, computers, and other library items). This will depend not only on the solo librarian's budget, but also the needs and wishes of the library's parent organization to provide additional security measures to ensure users' safety. The solo librarian and management should work closely to ensure that user safety is the primary goal here.

Solo librarians should also take an active role in working with their organizations to conduct emergency procedures and strategies for their institutions as a whole; not only does this involve solo librarians in actively participating in the community, but it also allows them to help maintain order, safety, and security throughout the institution.

Case studies

Amanda Tarbet, reference librarian, MGH Institute of Health Professions, Boston, MA

Information technology

I have an IT department that handles most troubleshooting issues. However, I do find myself in troubleshooting situations more often than I would like. For instance, I recently had to troubleshoot RefWorks. It turned out that the link we have to RefWorks in our CMS/website was causing problems because it was opening Refworks up inside the frame of the CMS. I needed to add a "target = _blank" to the link to ensure it would open in a new window/tab. We also occasionally have problems with Micromedex, a web app used widely by our nursing students for pharmaceutical info. And when we were choosing an ILS, the first one we chose had way too many troubleshooting issues, so we ended up going with Koha. I guess that most of my issues are software based, rather than hardware based, but it definitely helps to be comfortable with technology to be able to do troubleshooting. In 2007 I became a Mac person, and I do not do my own troubleshooting for my personal computer because I really don't understand Macs on that level. On the other hand, I have never had a virus or trojan since switching, so there's a trade-off there.

Library security

Safety and Security Policy

Although the MGH IHP Library is not a public library with a lot of traffic, it is nonetheless important to be aware of your surroundings. The building in which we are housed does get a great deal of guests/patients, and our floor is not locked during the day. Please adhere to the following procedures so that we may maintain a safe and welcoming environment for both the IHP community and guests.

General safety and security issues

Alerting staff to incidents

- When and how to call 911/MGH security
- Who to inform
- Filing reports/documentation

MGH security escorts

- How to request

Harassment by telephone, email, or in person

- What to do
- Who to inform
- If you are asked for your name

Log books

- Incident log
- Needs to be paper for signatures
- Should we be sending copies to MGH security?
- Log should be updated in a timely manner

Illness or injury

- Library does not provide first aid or medical assistance
- Who to contact if a patron/staff member is ill and needs assistance
- What to do if assistance is refused

Lost and found

- Lost and found items should be transferred to the first-floor security desk

Personal items

- Should be locked in desk and/or kept out of sight

Policies and training

- Policy should be reviewed annually
- Staff should be trained annually -- coordinate with MGH security?

Conduct of library users

The library is not a place for people to do whatever they want.

Rules violations: what to do if you need to approach a patron

- Remind of rules
- Give them an out

- Start nicely and become more authoritative if necessary
- Do not get into their space or touch them
- Call security if patron becomes aggressive or is under the influence of drugs and/ or alcohol

Computer violations

- All computers are under the administration of IT
- If you see a computer lab PC or laptop being misused, inform the IT help desk or other IT staff member

Emergency contacts

MGH security phone number:
Charlestown Navy security phone number:
Security desk in Building 36 phone number:

Lisa Lin, career resource consultant, McGill University Career Planning Services, Montreal, Quebec, Canada

Information technology

I'm lucky to have an IT department that does troubleshooting for us. All the staff computers are part of the university's computer domain and the basic security such as anti-virus and email filtering are all covered. The only thing I have to manage is the student computers, which are not part of the domain. I know a little about computer installation, and so far they haven't been a problem for me. For those who do install programs on their computers, a good website is http://ninite.com/. The site allows you to download the most commonly used free software (Essentials, Firefox, PDFCreator, FileZilla, etc.). The installation is pretty easy. Once you select a bunch of software programs, you get an installer that will install all the programs in one shot and does not require much interaction.

Some key issues that I also think are very important before buying:

- make sure the purchase fits your current and future computing needs
- find out what operating system (e.g. Windows XP) comes with the computer
- what peripherals are included with the computer.

In my case, I always pay attention to what operating system a computer comes with before buying. I try to choose a stable system that can last for a while (e.g. Windows XP rather than Vista), with the right peripherals (e.g. DVD drives and wireless network cards).

Library security

General Safety Guidelines

This section describes steps staff members should take when an incident is reported or takes place.

- General procedures
- Illness or injury
- *Lost and found*

Emergency Procedures

This section describes the emergency measures that will take place to ensure the safety of the community.

• Emergency evacuation
• Fire and smoke
• Medical emergencies
• Natural disasters

User Safety Guidelines

This section describes the Centre's expectations, users' responsibilities, and procedures to take to ensure safety.

• Cell phones
• Disruptive behavior
• Food and drink
• Library computers and printer
• Pets
• Suspicious behaviors
• Theft
• Sexual and other assaults
• Theft and vulnerabilities

Forms

• Disruptive behavior report
• Theft/loss report

Wendy O'Brien, Richmond Public Library, Richmond, VA

Library security

Draft Security Policy– Richmond Public Library

Security in building

• Keep all personal belongings in back room.
• Do not count book sale/fine money while patrons are present.
• Double-check all rooms (including back corners of non-fiction room and children's room as well as for problems in the bathroom) prior to closing.
• For the future: develop security incident form.

Security for computers

• See completed "Use of Patron Computers Policy".
• Always sign out of Library World to protect patron records.

Security for staff

• See completed "Unattended Child Policy".

- Be aware of front desk when helping patrons on computers or shelving books in back areas.
- For the future: install a mirror to help with security as well as providing assistance for handicapped entrance.

Carol Munroe, Milwaukee Public Schools, Milwaukee, WI

Information technology

Figure 5.2 is a very useful flowchart that can help solo librarians manage and trouble-shoot computer problems.

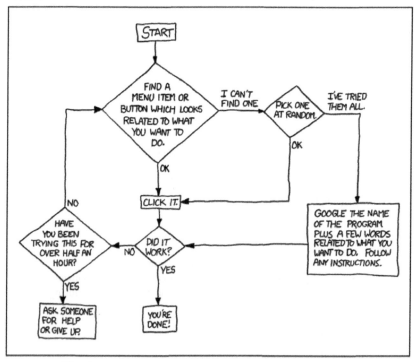

Figure 5.2 Flowchart of computer troubleshooting

Martha Kennedy, librarian, Concord Academy, Concord, MA

Library security

Security Plan for the J. Josephine Tucker Library

Facility Security

The Main School building, including the Library, is locked every evening and unlocked each morning by school security.

The Director staffs the Library from 7:30am–5:00pm, Monday through Friday. Evening staff coverage is provided from 6:00–9:00pm on Sunday, 7:00–9:30 on Monday, 6:30–9:30 on Tuesday and from 7:30–9:30 on Wednesday and Thursday. The building is opened each morning at 7:00am and secured once students return to their boarding houses by 10:00pm during the week, and 11:00pm on weekends.

The Library Office and workroom are locked until the Director arrives in the morning.

The school does not utilize video surveillance cameras on campus.

Collection Security

Signs are posted on each exit door clearly stating the Circulation Policies of the Tucker Library. A manual sign-out sheet is available on the Circulation Desk when the Director is away. All items are to be checked out at the desk.

Locked collections that require access with the Librarian are the DVD collection, the Alumni Authors case, and the Academy Archives.

The library does not utilize an alarm system for books.

Patron and Staff Security

Fire drills are conducted regularly through the school and the Town of Concord's Fire Department. Exits are clearly marked, and audible and visible alarms alert patrons to fire emergencies.

Furniture is safely maintained to allow easy egress to all exiting the facility.

Fire extinguishers are tested annually and are located throughout the facility.

Air-horn stations are also located throughout the facility and are to only be used to alert patrons of a lockdown drill or emergencies. The school's Director of Operations, in consultation with town emergency officials, has a clear plan that goes into place in the event of a lockdown situation. (This would be on the order of a dangerous person alert on the campus.)

In the event of a non-lockdown emergency, the Chapel bell rings continuously to call all to the Chapel for an all-community meeting. This would occur in the event of a 911-type incident.

Further explanation of our open campus policy in regards to campus buildings is in order. As a boarding/day school, approximately 40 per cent of our student and adult population live on campus. Ours is an open campus, meaning students do not need hall passes or permission to move about the campus when not enrolled in a class. This also means that students are free to walk into the town of Concord during free periods without explicit permission from an adult. If students are to leave campus by the commuter rail or by car, they must have permission to do so. With regard to open classrooms, studios, and common areas, the school's Code of Common Trust is the ruling principle. All community members are to treat all people's personal belongings with respect and not disturb, destroy, or take items belonging to others. This includes library items, classroom equipment, and dining-hall plates and cutlery. Overall, the amount of actual theft is quite low, but along with Common Trust goes its partner, Common Sense. Yes, materials do walk out of the library without being signed out or with my explicit permission, but that amount is small. In the years when full inventories were conducted, the general loss was well under 5 per cent. Some of the worst offenders are faculty, who often bury borrowed items in their offices for years. Students respond better to gentle cajoling or email reminders to return items. I'm also going to declare an amnesty day in which any taken items may be returned with no questions asked.

To summarize

- Solo librarians need to become computer and technology proficient to be able to assist their patrons with any questions they may have.
- Solo librarians need to be able to troubleshoot computers successfully so that, in the absence of any information technology professionals, they can keep their library computers well maintained and running smoothly.
- Solo librarians should compile ample resources to help patrons with information technology questions, and should stay current with the latest technologies.
- Solo librarians need to implement security strategies to maintain safety and security in their library spaces for their users.

Further reading

Bisson, Casey (2007). *Open-Source Software for Libraries*. Library Technology Reports. Chicago, IL: ALA Editions.

Courtney, Nancy D. (2005). *Technology for the Rest of Us: A Primer on Computer Technologies for the Low-Tech Librarian*. Santa Barbara, CA: Libraries Unlimited/ABC-CLIO.

Davis, Susan, Malinowski, Teresa, Davis, Eve, MacIver, Dustin, Corrado, Tina, and Spagnolo, Lisa (2012). "Who ya gonna call? Troubleshooting strategies for e-resources access problems". *Serials Librarian*, 62, 24–32.

Graham, Warren (2012). *The Black Belt Librarian: Real-World Safety & Security*. Chicago, IL: ALA Editions.

Halsted, Deborah D., Jasper, Richard P., and Little, Felicia M. (2005). *Disaster Planning: A How-To-Do-It Manual for Librarians*. New York: Neal-Schuman.

Kahn, Miriam B. (2008). *The Library Security and Safety Guide to Prevention, Planning, and Response*. Chicago, IL: ALA Editions.

Ratzan, Lee (2004). *Understanding Information Systems: What They Do and Why We Need Them*. Chicago, IL: ALA Editions.

Shuman, Bruce A. (2002). *Case Studies in Library Security*. Santa Barbara, CA: Libraries Unlimited/ABC-CLIO.

Cataloging and serials management

6

Cataloging

Cataloging is a task most librarians either love with a passion or hate with a passion. For those who have the luxury of having a cataloging department or a bookseller who completes all media cataloging for them, the task only arises with copy cataloging. However, most solo librarians either cannot afford to pay booksellers and vendors the cataloging processing fees or don't have the extra staff to assist with cataloging.

In any event, most one-person librarians will need to know (and review) the rudiments of cataloging, Figure 6.1 and Figure 6.2 whether it be Library of Congress or Dewey Decimal System, the two main cataloging classification systems. I should add that if a solo librarian uses his/her own classification system, he or she should stick to that and not be concerned about not using one of the two main systems; the important point here with cataloging for solo librarians is to ensure that their collection is organized properly and can easily be used by their patrons.

My first suggestion would be to take a crash course in cataloging and MARC records (if necessary) – this can usually be accomplished at a local library consortium or cooperative system, whether in person or online (for a nominal fee). The solo librarian can also use a meta-search website, such as the Internet Public Library (www.ipl. org) to find tutorials for both Library of Congress and Dewey Decimal classifications (Google and Wikipedia do have good resources as well, but will require, of course, a more detailed search to find reliable, useful, and current information on cataloging systems). A solo librarian can also use listservs, instant messaging, chat, and other online or in-person groups and organizations to learn cataloging classification systems.

I would also recommend creating a small library of cataloging books, such as Deborah Fritz's (2006) *Cataloging with AACR2 and MARC 21* (while a lengthy work itself, the Fritz binder is a much easier-to-use manual to catalog books, electronic resources, sound recordings, video recordings, and serials than with AACR2 or DDC), Michael Gorman's (2004) *The Concise AACR2*, Arlene Taylor's (2006) *Introduction to Cataloging and Classification*, Joseph Miller and Susan McCarthy's (2010) *Sears List of Subject Headings* (the authority text for DDC subject headings), and Lois Mai Chan's (2005) *Library of Congress Subject Headings* (the authority text on Library of Congress subject headings, in its most recent edition). These books will form a core reference collection that you can refer to for cataloging answers as the need arises.

The solo librarian also has electronic cataloging sources available; Baga et al. (2012) compiled what they call a "webliography" of current digital resources to assist librarians in the cataloging process.

Most one-person librarians have either inherited an OPAC with a specific cataloging software system or are in the process of buying one. Personally, I have never

Figure 6.1 Old card catalog: the "old" way to catalog

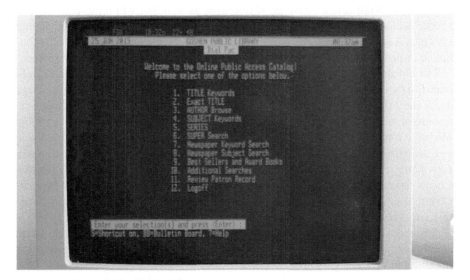

Figure 6.2 New card catalog: the "new" way to catalog

purchased any cataloging software, having inherited the OPAC software that my library used, but I have used several systems in my career and can offer the following rules of thumb.

- Most likely, your biggest purchase factors are cost and content; how much bang can you get for your buck?
- How often does the cataloging software need to be updated? Ideally, a solo librarian, given a limited budget, would want a system that does not need to be updated regularly and will remain useful and efficient as the collection increases in size.
- Do you choose a software-based system (such as Athena) or a web-based system (such as Auto-Graphics)? Both types have their merits and detractions (web-based systems usually do not have software bugs, but software systems are not at the mercy of internet bandwidth, overcapacity, or malfunctioning).
- How easy is copy cataloging – can you enter media with a few keystrokes, or does it involve the creation of a MARC 21 record?
- Finally, which software-based system do you (and your staff) find the easiest to use, the most comfortable to use, the easiest to learn?

What these considerations come down to are ease of use and reliability. Careful scrutiny of these software products (attending an ALA or state library conference exhibitors' hall is an investment worth considering) is paramount here.

Open-source library management software (such as Koha and NewGenLib) is now being used by a large number of librarians (Kamble et al., 2012), and has great potential for use by solo librarians, not only as it fits within their library budgets, but also it comes with a great range of uses and services that higher-priced library management software provides. As we will see with serials management, the push to save libraries (especially solo libraries) money in managing their resources should result in greater use of open-source software in the future.

Cataloging can be a chore, but it is a necessary and important task to ensure your patrons and students have proper access to library materials. With a little legwork (accomplished a bit at a time – remember the time management section of the book!), cataloging for the one-person library need not be a chore, but an important skill learned for an important task to complete and maintain as a solo librarian.

Serials management

Managing a serials collection is not an easy job, especially for the one-person librarian. Some libraries have a specific person assigned to this task, and of course there are many serials management services available, such as EBSCO, but how do you decide how to manage your serials collection? And where do you start?

First, take a step back and evaluate your serials collection, whether it is new or established. What magazines and journals are popular? How much space do you have available to display them? How much space do you have to store back issues? Which magazines and journals gather dust, unread and unused? This can be determined through a formal survey of patrons, students, instructors, and staff or by informal word of mouth (which can be the one-person librarian's friend for a quick and fairly accurate response!).

Budgeting is the next step – what serials deserve prominence in your library? Magazines, books, DVDs, or a bit of all three, for instance? Again, the answers to where to spend and what amount of materials to spend your money on lie in asking your students, patrons, and instructors what they deem are important resources for them. And then it is up to you, the librarian, to square the circle – to decide what is feasible, given the budget and space available to house the current and archived serials. It is an art and a science to juggle faculty or staff requests for periodicals with budget and space constraints, but only with practice, determination, diplomacy, and tact does a solo librarian succeed in creating a serials collection that pleases everyone, primarily the users.

Considering open access journals, through a website like Direct Open Access Journals (www.doaj.org) or the Public Library of Science (www.plos.org), can not only provide your users with current, relevant, and comprehensive articles across a wide spectrum of subjects, but also can be a life-saver on a solo librarian's budget. Lewis (2012) predicts that the majority of journal articles will be in open-source format by 2020; while no predictions will inevitably take place, the prohibitive cost of maintaining any serials collection, as well as dissemination of important research materials to users, will create a demand for a majority of materials to be supplied in open access format. These trends will allow solo librarians to provide a wider and more varied selection of periodicals for their users at a relatively low cost to their libraries.

Once your magazine and journal content is decided, do you manage the collection on your own, or do you hire a serials management agency? This, of course, depends on your budget and the size of your collection. The smaller your collection, the easier it is for you to manage on your own. But if your budget allows for a serials management company, you will find removing the hassles of chasing publishers for lost issues, for one thing, very liberating. Asking your colleagues about reliable companies is a very good idea – in addition, asking librarians who run similar libraries is a helpful, reassuring, and reliable yardstick to what serials management service is best for your library.

Now that you have your serials collection and serials management mapped out, how do you manage the magazines and journals once they are in your library? This depends on how you, as a one-person librarian, like to organize materials. Some librarians are content to enter new magazines longhand in a binder; other will create a barcode number for each individual magazine. And yet others will create an Access database or Excel spreadsheet to enter which journals arrive and when. The choice depends on your comfort level with technologies and organization.

What it comes down to, whether dealing with circulation or with weeding of periodicals, is your own comfort level and your library policies. Remember that technology can either be a hindrance or a help – it is a hindrance if it does not succeed in making your library more efficient and organized. Some of us (like myself) function more efficiently with paper and pen than with computers. But the correct answer lies with individual librarians, as it usually does.

Case studies

Amanda Tarbet, reference librarian, MGH Institute of Health Professions, Boston, MA

Cataloging

Our Community Health resources came from a library that is now closed, accompanied by a catalog in the form of an Excel spreadsheet and a unique classification system that is neither Dewey nor LCC [Library of Congress Classification] nor BISAC. It has been, well, a little frustrating dealing with the collection because of this, but we are muddling through.

So far, we have not done any cataloging. We are in the process of switching from the Excel sheet to an actual OPAC, and we are using the Koha ILS, which is open-source (but well-supported and active) ILS software. We are fortunate in that we have IT people to set Koha up for us. In that respect, it is technically free because the library is not paying for any of the server space or for the installation. However, if you are not server savvy and have some money, there are companies that will install and host Koha for you. I have no idea what they charge, but I think it depends on how big your library is. At any rate, I really like the software. Theoretically, copy cataloging will be easy once I get to that point because Koha can connect to other OPACs using the Z39.50 protocol (I think that is what it is called) and get records for me, which should (again, theoretically) make it easier for us eventually to switch to an LCC system.

Additionally, Koha can support RDA [resource description and access] cataloging, and I am seriously considering taking the RDA route since it'll be "official", or what have you, this year.

However, the nature of our collection means we have a lot of resources that will have no current catalog records to copy. This means that we will eventually have to do some original cataloging. What particularly interests me is the cataloging of "realia". We have, for instance, anatomical models that will need cataloging, and in my introductory cataloging class this was not something we covered. I will also have to look into cataloging things like posters, kits, and games. I'm excited to start learning!

Serials management

At the moment, my serials management duties are very minimal. Most of our journals are managed by the hospital library with which we are affiliated. We do have a few electronic serials subscriptions, however, that students currently access by using a universal username and password. I will be looking into what Koha can do for us for serials management, but for now the journals we manage are so few in number that we can keep track of them without additional software. Unfortunately, this means we have no usage statistics! Even though use is probably not very high because we are such a small school, you never know when some usage statistics might come in handy.

We are also keeping track of what journals our students ask for articles from through interlibrary loan, so that will help on the collection development side of things.

One thing that is particularly of interest to me is open access scholarly journals in the field of community health, and how to help make students aware of their existence. We don't have to subscribe, so they are not cataloged by us or the main hospital library. Thus far, I have relied on links through a LibGuide to point out their existence. However, I am considering adding them to the OPAC once I figure out how to work the serials management and how to catalog serials.

Lisa Lin, career resource consultant, McGill University Career Planning Service, Montreal, Quebec, Canada

Cataloging

As a career center with a small collection, we have our own classification system which I inherited from a previous librarian. We do not follow Dewey or LC classification. I have talked with other people who manage resources in a career center, and they all seem to have their own classification – some use numbers (e.g. 1.1 Career Description, 1.2 Job Search, etc.), others use A–Z format.

Having your own classification system has its own strengths and weaknesses. The strengths include:

- you don't have to worry about creating MARC records
- the books have a much shorter call number that makes sense to you and your users
- the books are shelved in a way that is logical for a career center, and users usually can locate books without difficulty (high browsability).

The weaknesses are:

- the classification is revised every year for expansion or contraction
- the cataloguing system has to be custom-made – in my case, our IT developed a customized cataloging system.

Serials management

I have a small library with very few periodicals. The weeding policy is very simple: magazines/newspapers that are more than two years old are either put in the give-away box or the recycle bin. This policy is relevant to an article I found online, "Weeding tips: the basics" (www.booklistonline.com/ProductInfo.aspx?pid = 5346510). The article offers a few basic rules as a guideline to weed materials: M – misleading; U – ugly; S – superseded by a new edition; T – trivial (of no discernible literary or scientific merit); I – irrelevant; E – elsewhere (the material is easily obtainable).

In my case:

- the periodicals contain job listings and they become irrelevant to users after a while (the rule of I – irrelevant)
- the periodicals have a free online edition which can be easily retrieved from the publishers' websites (the rule of E – elsewhere).

In addition, due to the limited shelf space, I simply cannot afford to store all the periodicals for a long time.

To summarize

- Cataloging and serials management are skills that solo librarians need to possess in order to manage and maintain their research resources for their users.
- Various strategies, including the use of open-source and open access software, will allow solo librarians to provide a wide range of electronic resources and cataloging within their library budgets.

If your library has a current copy of AACR or DDC, I commend you; your cataloging library is complete. But the easier-to-read and easier-to-use resources listed at the end of this chapter may be of more use to a solo librarian. Also, I searched several of the scholarly journals in this area, such as *Cataloging and Classification Quarterly*, and found many of the articles a bit too overwhelming and esoteric to use for solo librarians. Again, the following resources are more likely to be useful than academic articles.

References

Baga, John, Hoover, Lona, and Wolverton, Robert E. (2012). "Online, practical, and free cataloging resources: an annotated webliography". *Library Resources & Technical Services*, *57*(2), 100–117.

Chan, Lois Mai (2005). *Library of Congress Subject Headings* (4th edn). Santa Barbara, CA: Libraries Unlimited/ABC-CLIO.

Fritz, Deborah A. (2006) *Cataloging with AACR2 and MARC* (21). (2nd edn). Chicago, IL: ALA Editions.

Gorman, Michael (2004). *The Concise AACR2* (4th edn). Chicago, IL: ALA Editions.

Kamble, V. T., Raj, Hans, and Sangeeta (2012). "Open source library management and digital library software". *DESIDOC Journal of Library & Information Technology*, *32*(5), 388–392.

Lewis, David (2012). "The inevitability of open access". *College & Research Libraries*, *91*, 493–506.

Miller, Joseph, and McCarthy, Susan (2010). *Sears List of Subject Headings* (20th edn). New York: H.W. Wilson.

Taylor, Arlene (2006). *Introduction to Cataloging and Classification* (10th edn). Library and Information Science Text Series. Santa Barbara, CA: Libraries Unlimited/ABC-CLIO.

Further reading

Black, Steve (2006). *Serials in Libraries: Issues and Practices*. Santa Barbara, CA: Libraries Unlimited/ABC-CLIO.

Bluh, Pamela M. (2001). *Managing Electronic Serials*. Chicago, IL: ALA Editions.

Chen, Chou-Sen Dora (1995). *Serials Management: A Practical Guide*. Chicago, IL: ALA Editions.

Davis, Susan, Feick, Tina, England, Deborah, Aipperspach, Jeff, Steinle, Kim, Beckett, Chris, and Holley, Beth (2010). "Navigating your way through the e-journal rapids". *Serials Librarian*, *58*(1/4), 5.

Freeland, Marija, and Bailey, Marcia (2008). "Print newspapers: are they still being used in academic and research libraries?" *Serials Librarian*, *55*(1/2), 210.

Hrions, Jean and Reynolds, Regina (1999) "Seriality: it's not just for serials anymore". *Library Review, 48*(4): 163–169. A slightly long article, but focus on the bullet-point recommendations; they are a useful reference for serials and cataloging management.

O'Doherty, Sean, and Boissy, Bob (2009). "Is there a future for the traditional subscription-based journal?" *Serials Librarian*, *56*(1/4), 155–162.

Stamison, Christine, Persing, Bob, Beckett, Chris, and Brady, Chris (2009). "What they never told you about vendors in library school". *Serials Librarian*, *56*(1/4), 139–145.

Staffing the one-person library

7

As I wrote in my preface to this book, one of the main reasons why I became a solo librarian was to manage my own library, without assistance from other staff or librarians. This, of course, does not mean that I dislike working with other librarians or staff, but rather it is because I enjoy managing a library on my own and being responsible for all my duties and activities as a solo librarian. In addition, as a solo librarian I have fairly wide latitude to create my own library programs and procedures for my students, staff, and faculty (of course, with guidance of management, as well as within educational parameters or guidelines); being able to create your own methods of disseminating research and information to your users is a very positive and strong reason to become a solo librarian, despite running a library by yourself. But sometimes solo librarians do need to assess whether they can manage and run things by themselves, and may need to staff their libraries to ensure that users will always be able to find assistance. This is especially true if your library's operating hours run past usual daytime opening into the evening, and coverage by one person is not feasible or possible. This is also the case if solo librarians need to work on a project that takes them away from their desks or have to teach information literacy classes; their other responsibilities as librarians can be stretched thin and leave them unable to assist all of their users at the same time. For this reason, a solo librarian may want to staff the library to maintain its operations; closing down a library, in the circumstances mentioned above (or others), is not an option for any solo librarian or solo library (unless an emergency occurs, of course). What are the staffing options for solo librarians, and how can staff, if obtained, be trained successfully to assist so they can provide the best service possible for the library's users?

Staffing strategies for solo librarians

Assessing the need for library staff

Before considering hiring any staff, a solo librarian should sit down, first alone and then with his/her manager, to determine the need for staff. Questions about staffing can include the following.

- Does the library need staffing to ensure users receive the best service and assistance possible?
- What hours of the day are the critical times for additional staff coverage?
- How many additional staff members should be hired to ensure users receive the best service and assistance?
- What funds are available to pay for additional staff, or can volunteers be recruited for positions?
- How much training will staff require to work in the library and provide the best service possible to the library's users?

Once these questions have been answered in detail and agreement reached with management, the solo librarian can begin to recruit staff; the type of staff hired will, of course, depend on the answers to these questions by the librarian and the organization's management.

Volunteers

If solo librarians need additional staff for their libraries, they can take the example of what many public libraries do if they need more staff – recruit volunteers. A solo librarian can, as a strategy, contact a public library's friends group or other voluntary group and inquire if any of the members wish to volunteer in a one-person library. Or they may know of others not involved in the public library groups who may wish to volunteer to work in the one-person library. If a solo librarian manages a medical library, s/he can potentially hire staff from a hospital's volunteer group or organization. An academic solo library can hire either work-study students (if they are available) or graduate library school students to work as part of an internship or cooperative employment program in conjunction with their graduate school. The solo librarian can also use various forms of social media, such as Twitter, LinkedIn, or Facebook, to hire volunteers as staff members. The main point here is that no matter what type of library a solo librarian manages, s/he can find volunteer staff to help run it smoothly and efficiently.

Paid staff and internships

If solo librarians do have funds to pay for library staff, where can they find potential recruits? The internet and social media provide many easy, cost-effective methods to locate the best people for staffing a one-person library, but as mentioned above with regard to volunteers, solo librarians can use strategies beyond internet advertising and want ads to staff their libraries.

The best source of staff can be graduate students in library and information science; these students have a wealth of knowledge from their courses and can apply that knowledge to assisting the solo librarian in managing and running a one-person library successfully. Another positive aspect of graduate students is their various backgrounds and specializations with regard to libraries; they may be familiar with the workings of law libraries, medical libraries, or school media centers, for instance. A solo library with staffing needs can easily and effectively ask management for a small stipend to fund an internship for potential staff, given that these graduate students, with their background and experience, can assist the solo librarian successfully in serving the library's users. This not only helps the library; it also allows graduate students to gain valuable experience in their on-the-job training. From my personal experience, in my last year of graduate school I worked as a paid intern for one year in a special library that dealt with information technology. Not only did I assist with cataloging and checkout of library materials, but I answered in-depth research questions sent to the library from the various branch offices. This valuable experience enabled me to accept my first full-time librarian position shortly after my internship ended. Organizations, if they have enough foresight and funds, can enable solo librarians to hire professional interns to assist them in running their libraries; it is a win-win situation for both, as solo librarians will have managerial assistance from professional library students and library students will gain valuable experience that will help them in their future careers.

Training staff

Training new staff need not be a challenge or a chore, but in practice each library has different policies and procedures that must be followed. Solo librarians need to familiarize their staff with these policies and procedures so they are familiar with how the library functions. If a solo librarian is lucky enough to have a staff member who is a library graduate student proficient in cataloging and cataloging databases, or a volunteer who is proficient in computers and IT troubleshooting, for instance, the librarian will be able to allow them to become responsible for their area of expertise. Solo librarians should also take advantage of numerous webinars and free tutorials (such as those found on www.microsoft.com for computer and IT training), so that their staff can become knowledgeable in these areas. Local library consortia or library associations also offer free or low-cost webinars throughout the year, so training can be held continuously and not just at one time of year. And this is the important point about training – it never ends and should never be held at a regular time during the year. Training needs to be done constantly and as often as possible, to ensure that staff (and the solo librarian) remain current in their knowledge of library management, trends, strategies, and skills.

Assessing staff

Most solo librarians, in the end, hire very capable staff to help them manage their libraries, but even the most dedicated and conscientious staff need to have regular assessments to ensure they are performing their tasks properly, effectively, and efficiently. These can consist of formal, regular meetings (quarterly, for instance) to discuss how the staff member is performing and what is expected for him or her in the future (with written documentation of the meeting, and the information placed in the staff member's personal file); the solo librarian can also offer the staff member a short survey to complete to find out how s/he is doing and any improvements (or commendations) that need to be made to the staff member's work history.

No staff members are perfect or exemplary workers, and some disciplinary issues may arise in the library. The solo librarian, in most cases, will work with his/her manager in the organization to follow and conduct the organization's disciplinary guidelines for staff members. If the solo librarian does not have a manager, s/he will have to follow and carry out the disciplinary guidelines and procedures alone. It is hoped that it will be a simple and quick procedure to remove a staff member who is causing trouble or having work issues, but only with experience does this task become easier.

One bright side to this difficult process is that the solo librarian learns new management skills along the way; that is the way that any solo librarian becomes a good manager of people as well as of procedures and policies.

To summarize

- Solo librarians may need to hire, and should seriously consider hiring, additional staff to assist them in managing their libraries.
- There are a good and vast variety of methods of finding and hiring library staff within a solo librarian's budget.
- Library staff should be recruited and hired with specific skills sets in mind (such as computer troubleshooting) to assist the solo librarian in managing the library in the best manner possible.
- Library staff should be assessed regularly to ensure they are performing their tasks efficiently and effectively.

Further reading

Giesecke, Joan (2010). *Fundamentals of Library Supervision* (2nd edn). Chicago, IL: American Library Association.

Nicol, Erica A., and Johnson, Corey M. (2008). "Volunteers in libraries: program structure, evolution and theoretical analysis". *Reference & User Services Quarterly*, *48*(2), 154–163.

Quinney, Kayla L., Smith, Sara D., and Galbraith, Quinn (2010). "Bridging the gap: self-directed staff technology training". *Information Technology & Libraries*, *29*(4), 205–213.

Wigbels Stewart, Andrea, Washington-Hoagland, Carlette, and Zsulya, Carol T. (eds) (2013). *Staff Development: A Practical Guide* (4th edn). Chicago, IL: ALA Editions.

Final thoughts on solo librarianship and the future of solo librarians   8

As I mentioned in my introduction to the book, why did I write this book? I wrote this book so that solo librarians would have a guide to managing and maintaining their libraries effectively and efficiently; not all solo librarians can enroll in my original online continuing education course, and even if they did so, they would need to book to refer to once the course ends if they have any questions or concerns to resolve. A book, whether in print or in electronic form, serves as a good resource to use once a class ends when library concerns arise (and there will always be problems to solve!) This is especially true for solo librarians and paraprofessionals, since they manage their libraries and are also the person many in an organization turn to for assistance and guidance in solving their problems. Of course, one manual cannot serve as the exact or perfect guide for every librarian and for every library, but I believe, when I created this online course and I decided to write this book, that I can impart some of my experience managing one-person libraries and solo librarians and paraprofessionals can take that knowledge and use it towards their own goals and towards their own ends. In effect, they can take what knowledge others have acquired and applied to their own ends, and tailor that knowledge and experience to each solo librarian's ends. And that is what solo librarians and paraprofessionals need to do; they need to be resourceful and find methods and strategies to manage their libraries on their own with limited funds and budgeting. A solo librarian needs to acquire skills to learn to be a juggler of time and resources, as well as become all things to all people where they work, as in many institutions, they are the information professionals and have the answers or resources other staff require for their work. They must continually learn new skills and strategies, through their professional development in learning in print and on the web, to enable their libraries to continue to become an information hub, so to speak, for all their users.

What is an information hub? It is a place where a user can find the information he or she is looking for, as well as provide a place for conducting research and study; this mainly consists of using print material and electronic database material, but it also consists of the solo librarian's compiled knowledge and wisdom they have accumulated through experience at their work on what materials to use and where to find them. They are teachers as well as information disseminators. Given the presence of the World Wide Web and the computer, users find themselves deluged with information that they may not be able to successfully sort and use properly; a librarian can assist them to navigate this confusing, yet information-rich, electronic world to find the information they can use to answer their question. And, they can teach them the skills that they will need to find information when they search and use databases and other resources in the future.

This leads into an important question: do libraries, especially solo libraries, matter in this digital age, where we can find answers to our questions with a click of a mouse and an Enter key? The answer is yes; the human component, in the form of any type of librarian, will always be a part of any library. You can have a fully digital library, with no print books, full of the latest electronic databases, electronic books and other digital information, but they are useless without the knowledge and guidance of a librarian, an information professional who can not only guide users to the information, but teach them how to use it. Given many libraries' budgets, and the needs and wishes of their users, many libraries, I believe, will become (if they are not already) hybrid libraries, with a balanced blend of both print and electronic research resources. This is the crucial place where solo librarians need to stay ahead of the technology curve and learn how to not only use new technologies, but discern which ones will function best in their library for their user's needs. They also need to be knowledgeable and remain current with their collection development policies so that their print and serial resources remain current and reliable resources for their users. Finally, solo librarians need to have superlative, exemplary teaching skills to help their users how to navigate these electronic resources, users will either need guidance and assistance when a new database arrives or just need continued assistance with the current digital resources. And a librarian will be there to assist them to find the information they are looking for, as well as get them started to learning how to use the library's research resources for themselves, and to maintain these resources for currency and reliability. We have not yet arrived at the time when robots will assume librarians' responsibilities to help their users find information, but it is a safe bet to assume that most users will want to have a knowledgeable, helpful, and resourceful human being to assist them in finding the information that they need. Librarians of all types need to realize this important insight when they need to explain to their managers or supervisors for their continued presence in any organization.

And this is especially true for solo librarians, given smaller operating budgets for resources, to mention one crucial aspect of running a successful library. Solo librarians will have to deal with maintaining current, accurate and reliable resources for their users under these constraints in order to succeed, and it is my hope that this book will be a helpful guide to those solo librarians and paraprofessionals who want to learn how to continue to offer their research and resources services to their users in the best ways that they can do so. Solo librarianship is not an easy task, but by using this book as a guide, and then using their own experience and knowledge taken from their specific libraries, they will have the tools to make their task a bit easier for them to provide the best research resources possible for their users, and, just as important, thrive and enjoy their work as solo librarians.

Useful websites

Direct Open Access Journals – www.doaj.org
Free software – http://ninite.com/
Internet Public Library – www.ipl.org
Microsoft – www.microsoft.com
Public Library of Science – www.plos.org
Teach Yourself Visually book series – www.wiley.com/compbooks
Terms of Service Didn't Read – www.tosdr.org

Index

Edwards Brothers Malloy
Ann Arbor MI. USA
December 23, 2014